SERGIO ARAGONÉS

MAD

AS THE DEVIL!

Albert B. Feldstein, Editor

WARNER BOOKS

A Warner Communications Company

WARNER BOOKS EDITION

This Warner Books Edition is published by
arrangement with E.C. Publications, Inc.

Warner Books, Inc., 75 Rockefeller Plaza, New York, N.Y. 10019

A Warner Communications Company

Printed in the United States of America

First Printing: March, 1975

Reissued: December, 1981

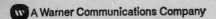

TO MY FRIENDS IN MEXICO: JULIO ALVARADO * ARNALDO COEN * OSCAR PLIEGO * GUSTAVO SAINZ * SILVIA LEMUS * RAMON VALDIOSERA * RAUL PEREZ PRIETO * OSCAR GALEANO * PACO ROMERA * ELVIRA CASTILLO * ALFREDO GIL * RIUS * JUAN MARTINEZ * ARTURO LOMELI * PEPE DIAZ * SERGIO AJURIA * RUBEN BROIDO RODOLFO ECHEVERRIA * LUIS LOPEZ LOSA * PEPE GUTIERREZ * HUMBERTO JURADO LEE BURNETT * CARLOS ENRIQUE TABOADA * JORGE CASARIN * HECTOR ORTEGA RENE CARDONA * OCTAVIO BAROCIO * JUAN LOPEZ MONTEZUMA * NACHO MENDEZ ALEJANDRO JODOROWSKY * JOSE ALVAREZ C. * MARTA PALAU * JUAN IBAÑEZ * P.I.T. PEPE ESTRADA * RAFAEL CORONEL * LUIS MARRASE * JUAN VOLLRATH * PACO ICAZA CARLOS FUENTES * ALBERTO ISAAC * PEPITA GOMIS * RAUL DE ANDA * JAIME VIDAL MODESTO BORONAT * ROBERTO DONIS * ANTONIO GONZALEZ DE LEON * ALFONSO ARAU VICTOR FOSADO * PILAR ALCALA * EDUARDO MATA * AURORA MOLINA * CHALO LAITER ARTURO RIPSTEIN * GELSEN GAS * HECTOR VOLLRATH * JAVIER SOLANA * HOMERO ARIDJIS * BRIAN NISSON * RENE REBETEZ * ROSA FURMAN * JACK WINER * SERGIO JURADO * FERNANDO MACOTELA * HELEN BICKHAM * ARNALDO LUCCI * ANTONIO IBARRA * CARLOS MONSIVAIS * MONSE, ANA MARIA Y MARIA TERESA PECANINS * ALBERTO DALLAL * TONI SBERT * LORENA VINIEGRA * OSCAR CHAVEZ * MARTA PALAU * CARMEN CIRICI * ANTONIO ESPINOSA * FELIPE EHREMBERG * ALBERTO LEDUC * JORGE BAUCHE * VICENTE ROJO * GEORGES MASSART * GERMAN ROBLES GILBERTO ESCOBEDO * LEONORA CARRINGTON * AUGUSTO BONDANI * HECTOR SUAREZ DAVID ALKON * MANOLO ESPINOSA * PANCHO CORZAS * IGNACIO MARQUEZ * MANUEL ALDECOA * TITO BAUCHE * CONCHITA SOLANA * MANUEL ARAGONES * HIRAM GARCIA BORJA * JOSE LUIS CUEVAS * ENRIQUE VOLLRATH * JULIA VILLASEÑOR ENRIQUE ROCHA * LUIS ARIZA * ANTONIO BALMORI * LA MARKOVA * JULIAN PASTOR PIRULI * GUILLERMO MENDIZABAL * MARTA ZAVALETA * ALEJANDRO PARODI * CHANO VEJAR * LUIS GUILLERMO PIAZZA * BARBARA WASSERMAN * JUAN JOSE GURROLA MARIA LUISA MENDOZA * LOS GARCIA FRADE * TOMAS AUÑON * HECTOR AZAR RAUL KANFFER * CARMEN ESPINOSA * CHUCHO RODRIGUEZ * RICARDO ROCHA J. MUÑOZ DE BAENA * MAGDA DE HOYOS * GUSTAVO OLGUIN * JAVIER ORDOÑEZ JACK MISRACHI * EDMUNDO ARAGONES * TATIANA GORIOLI * RODOLFO DE ANDA MARIO MOYA PALENCIA * LINDA VINIEGRA * POLO GOUT * MARIA RODRIGUEZ JOSE LUIS GONZALEZ DE LEON * MAURICIO HERRERA * ALBA CAMA * DANIEL CASTRO DEL VALLE * ROGELIO NARANJO * LEONARDO VADILLO * TATEI HICURI * CARLOS BAILLET * JOSE LUIS SAINZ * THOMAS FORTSON * SONIA FURIO * MAURICIO SORIANO ALFREDO VILANA * VICTOR M. CASTELL DE ORO * ENRIQUE GONZALEZ VILLALVA * MOISES CADRON DE GUEVARA * JOSE LUIS CARO * RICARDO ALBA * ANTONIO FLORES LUIS M. OLAVARRIETA * MANUEL FELGUEREZ * MANUEL CARDOSO * ANTONIO DIAZ CARLOS AROUESTY * PEDRO SOL * TUNO ALVARENGA * JULIO PELLISSER * ANGEL ZAMARRIPA * GENARO HURTADO * MANUEL ESPINOSA * AGUSTIN ESPINOSA * SERGIO DE YTURBE * EMILIO GARCIA RIERA * ALEX PHILLIPS JR. * GASTON MELO OFELIA MEDINA * OTHON SANCHEZ * LOS PELAEZ * RAUL MORALES * ALDO MONTI PEDRO ARMENDARIZ * JACOBO ZABLUDOWSKY * ALBERTO MARTINEZ * ROSSAS

WHO I MISS VERY MUCH!

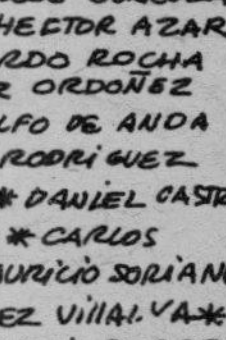

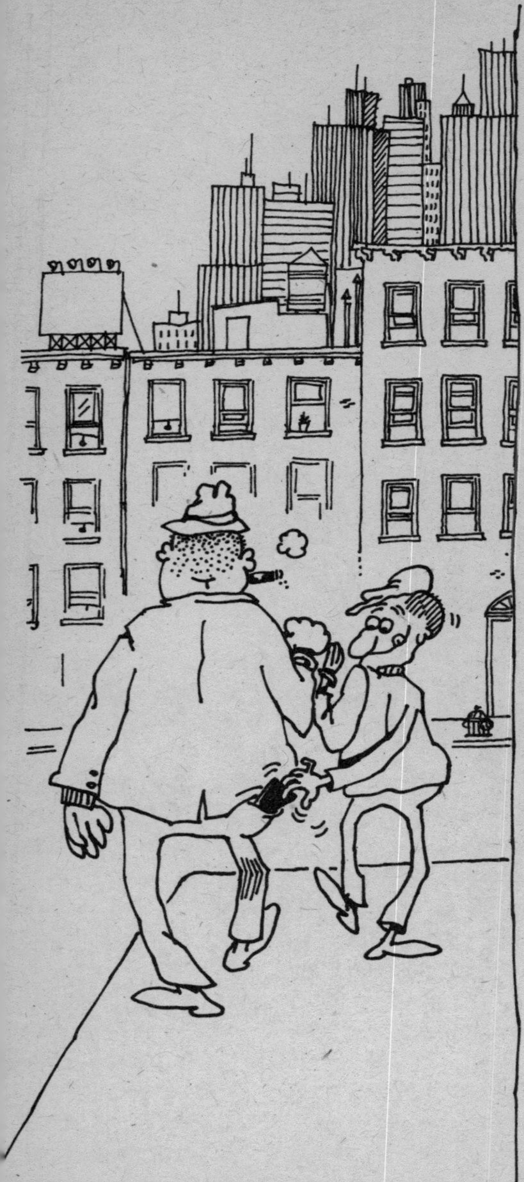

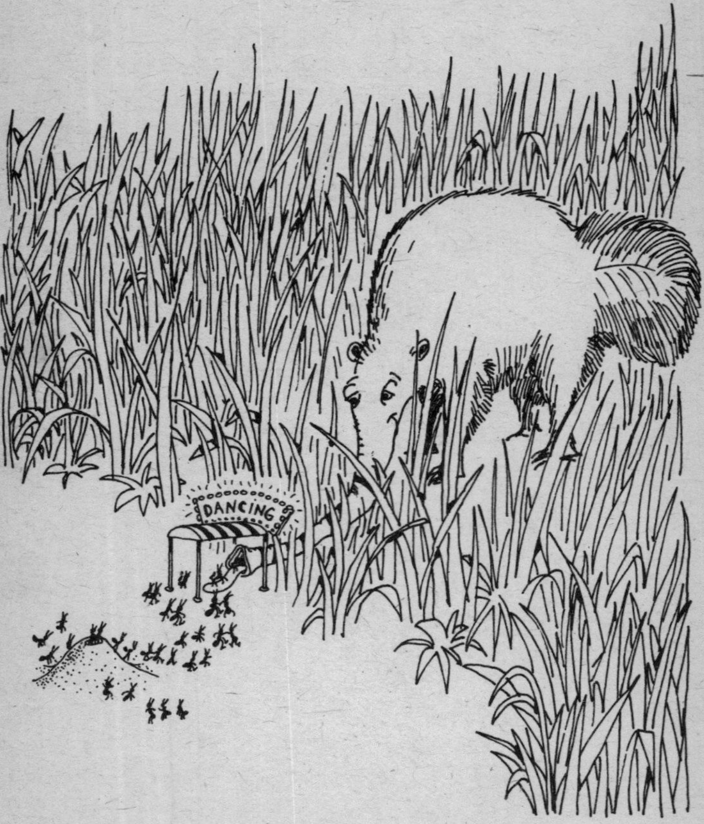
DANCING

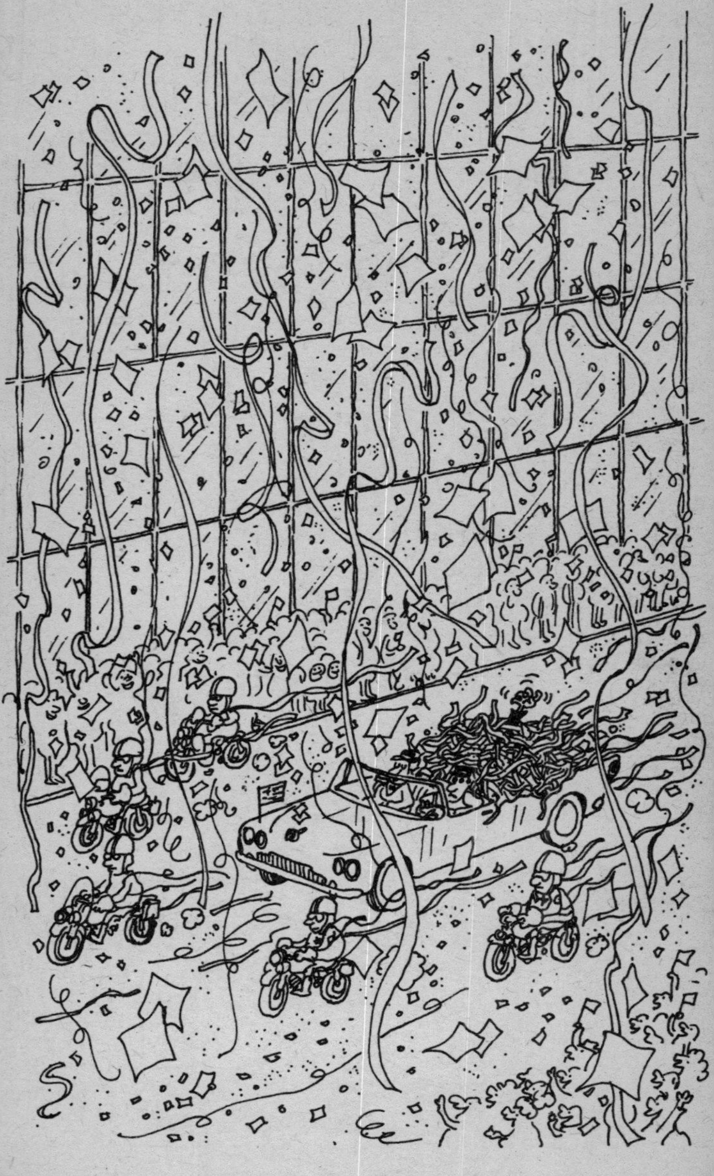

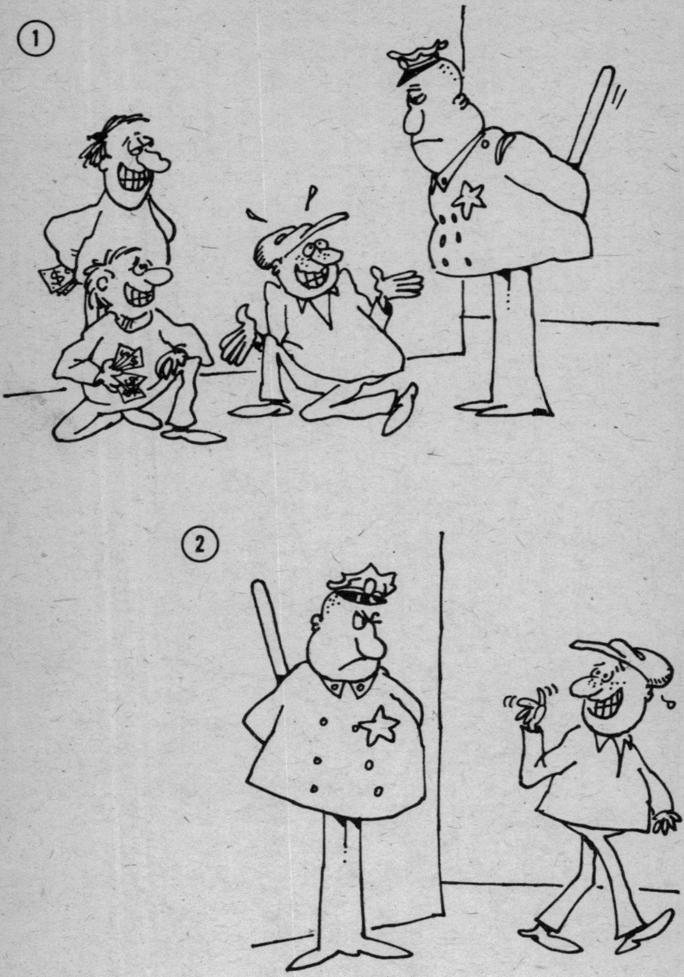
1
2

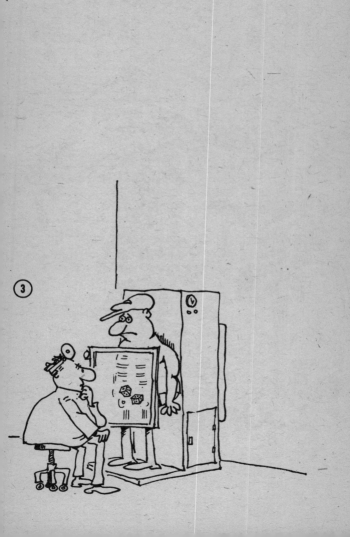

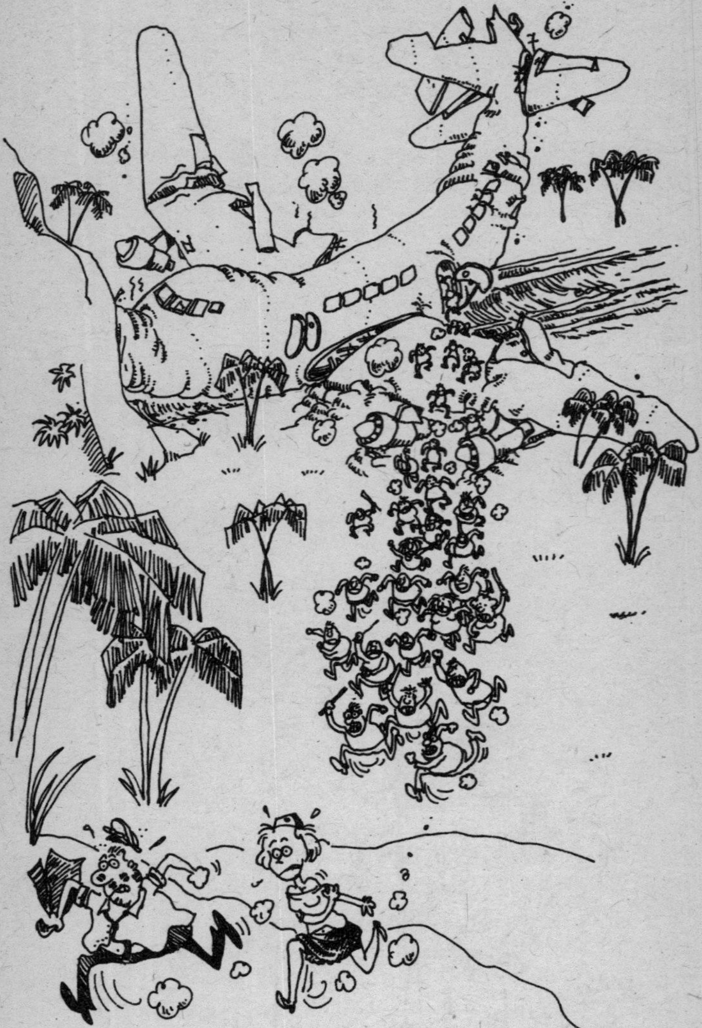

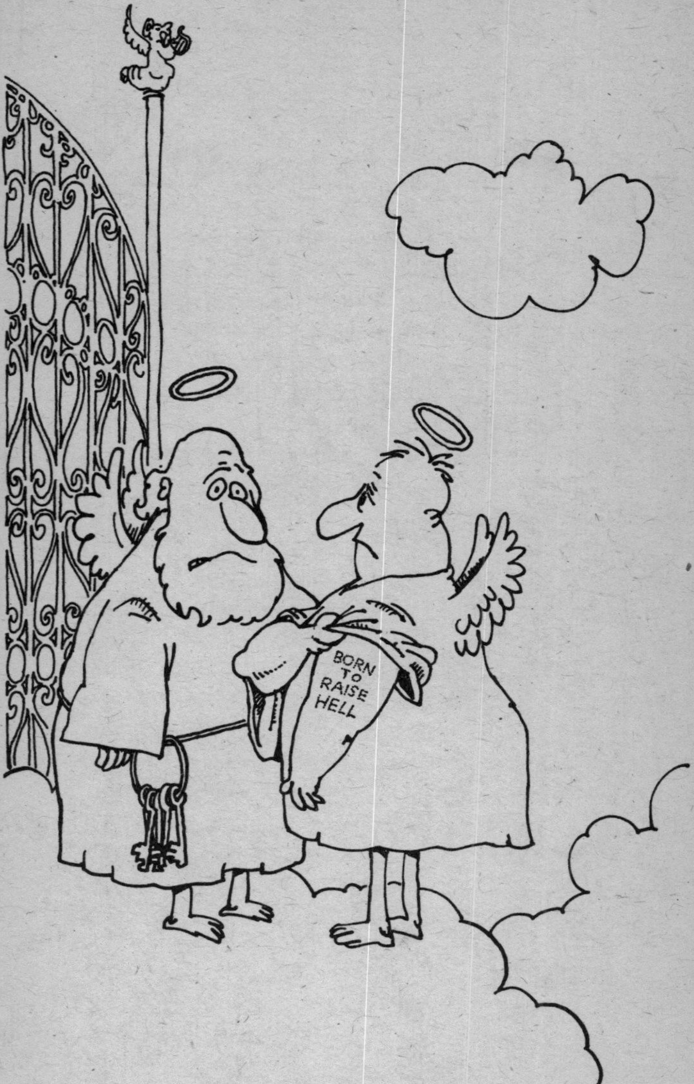
BORN TO RAISE HELL

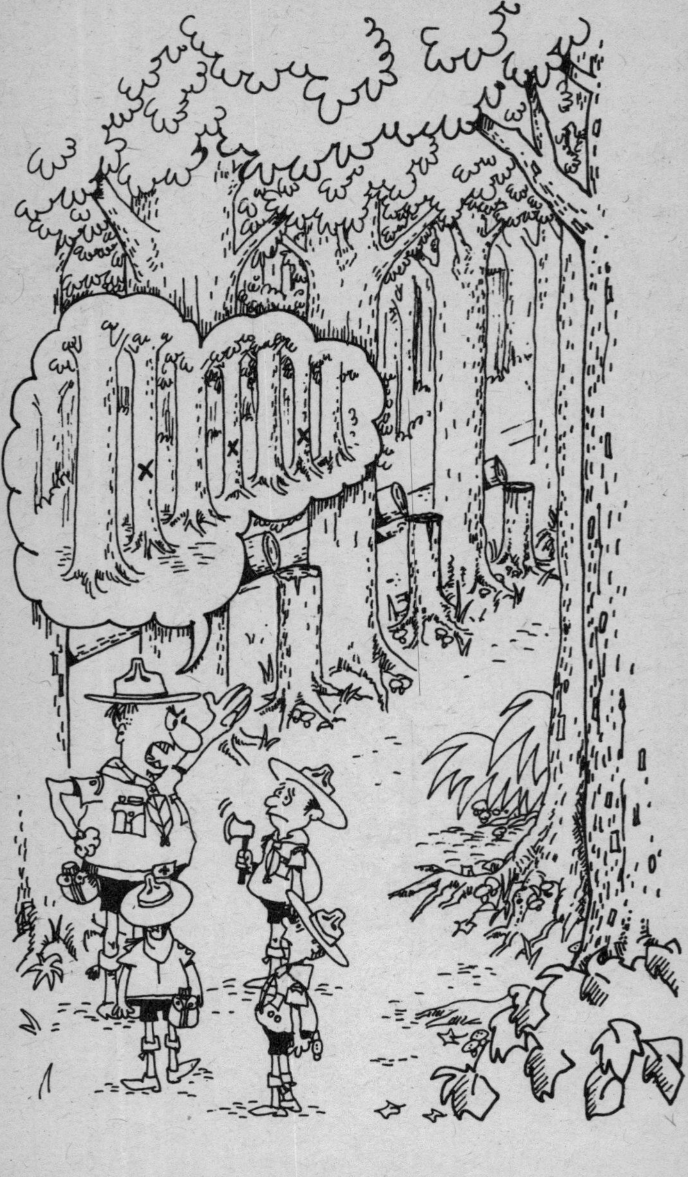

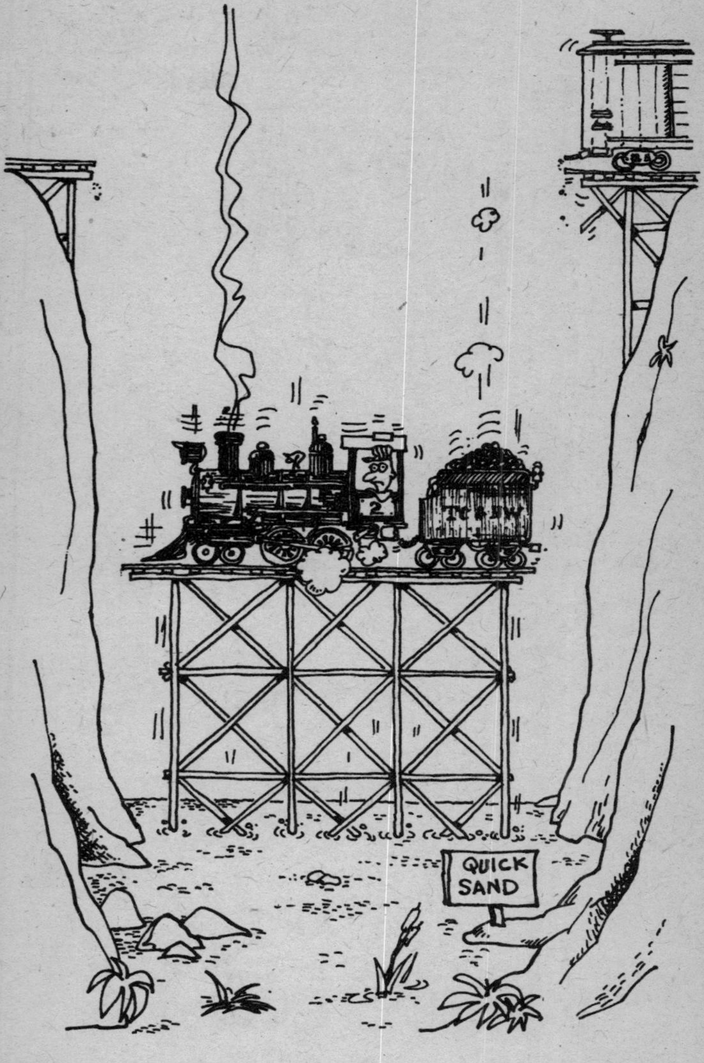
QUICK
SAND

1

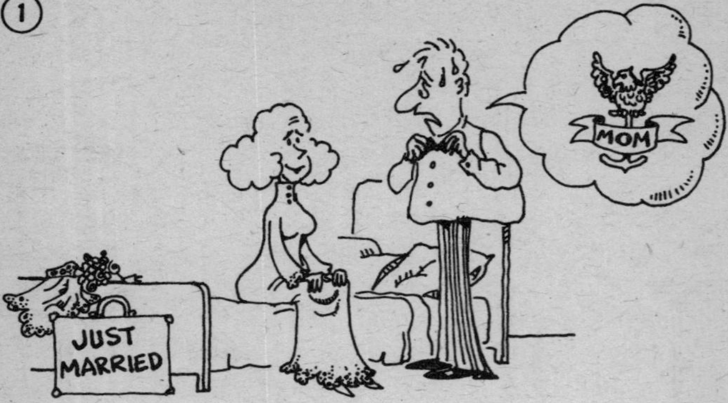
MOM
JUST
MARRIED

2

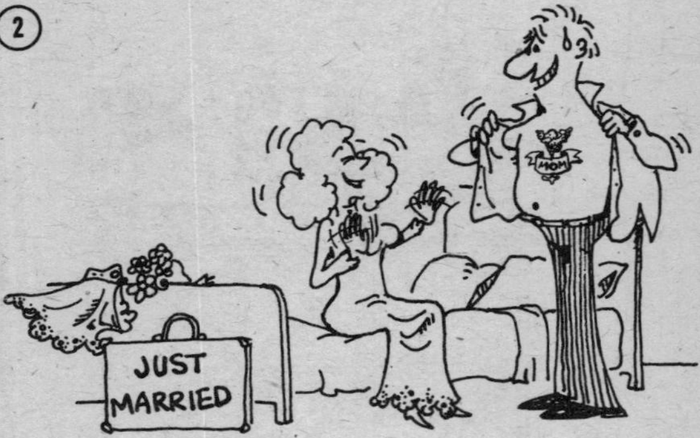
MOM
JUST
MARRIED

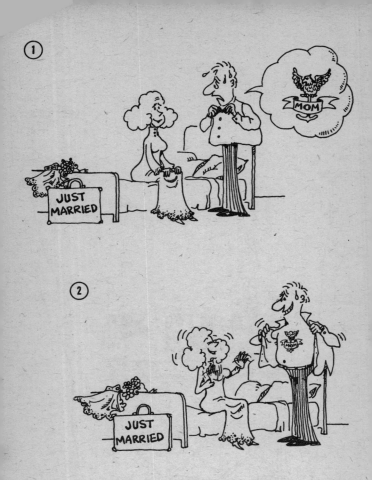

3

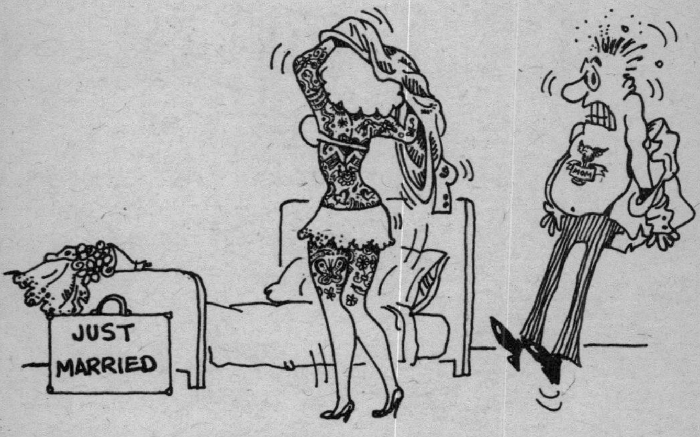

JUST
MARRIED
MOM

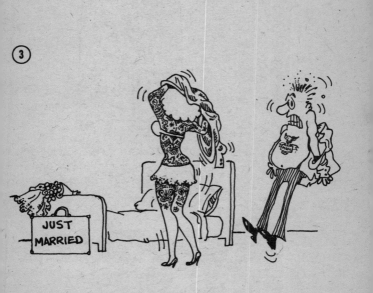

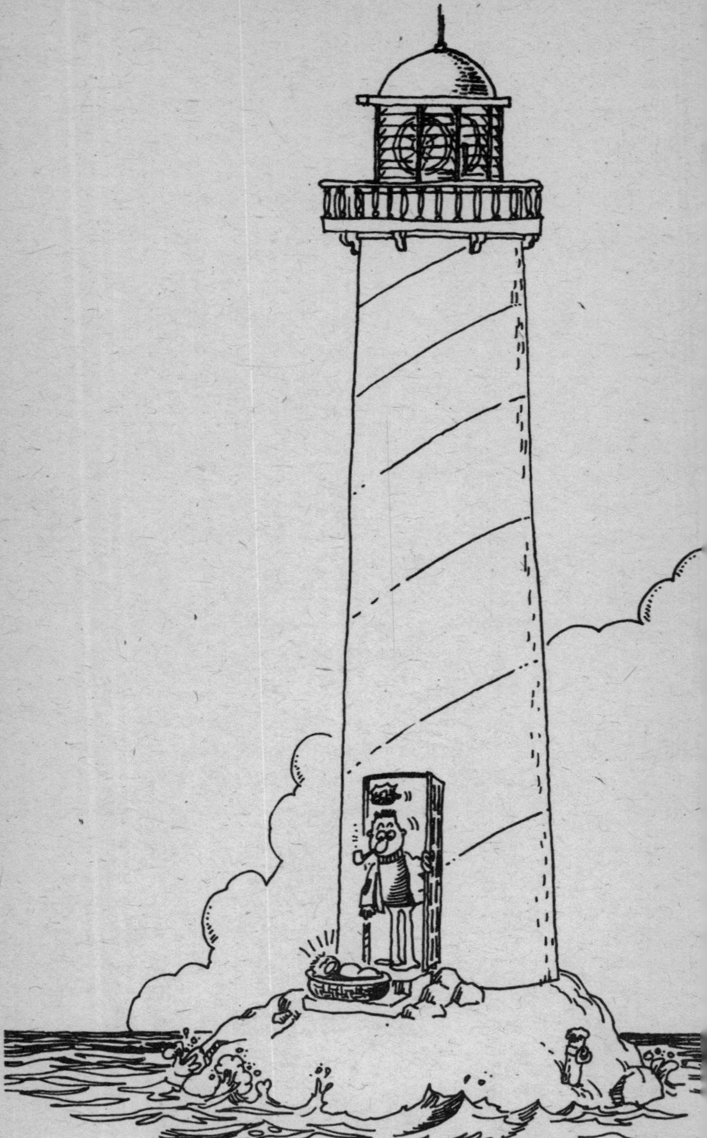

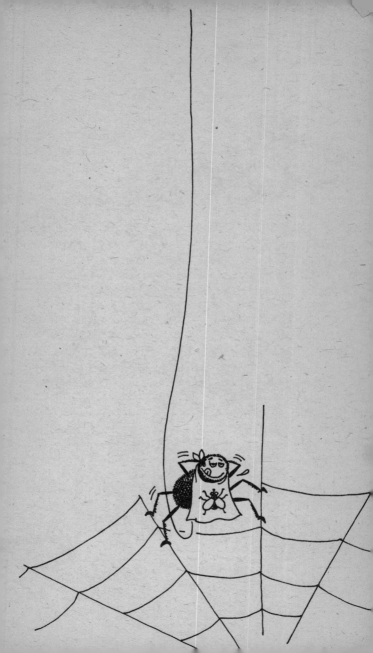

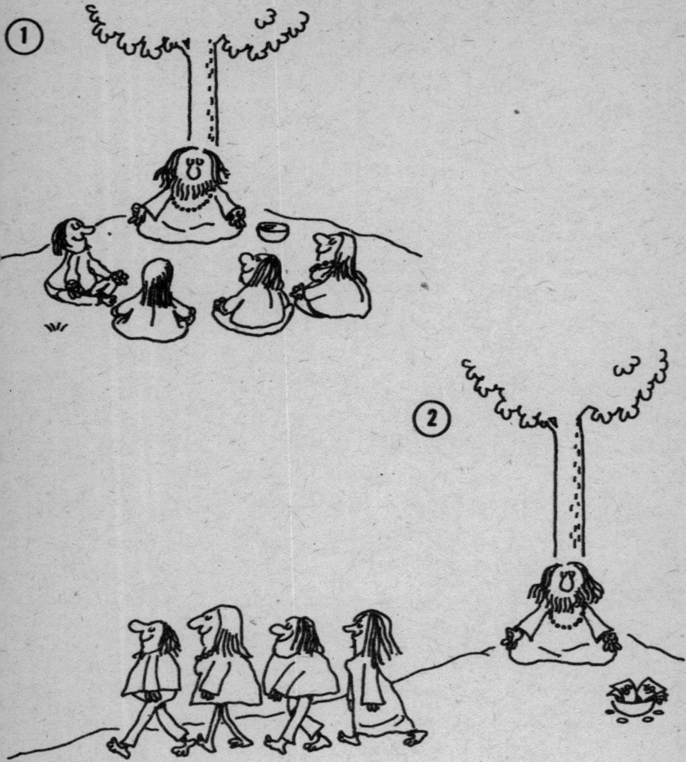
1
2

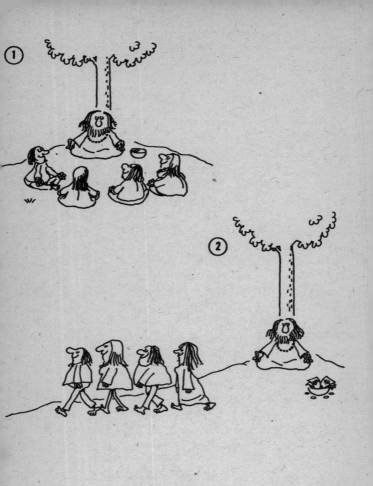

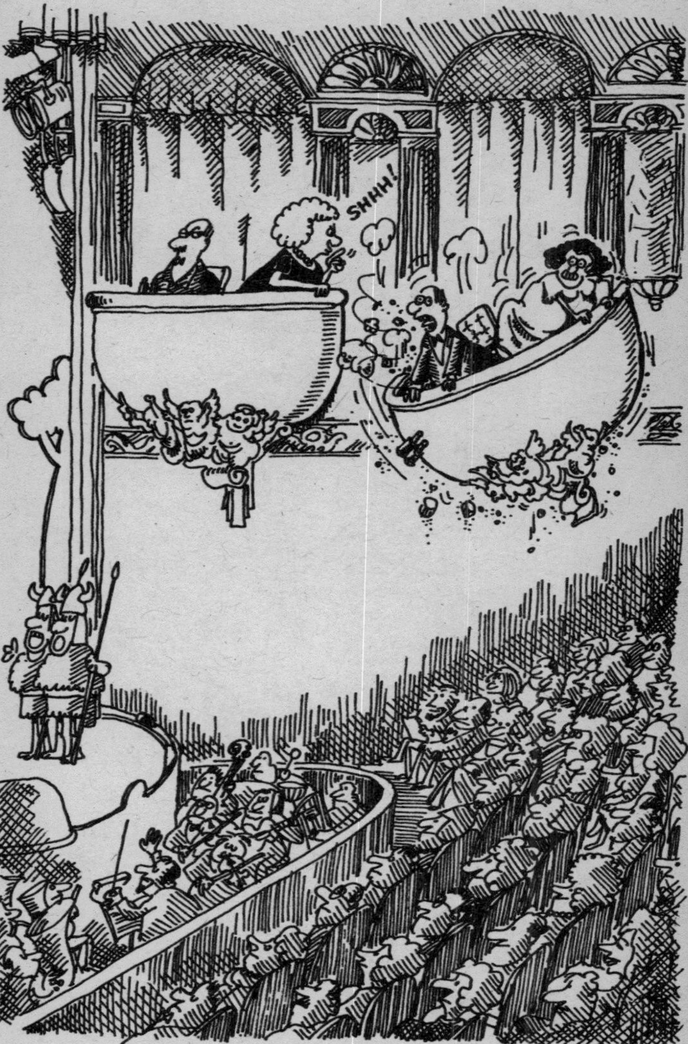
SHHH!

1

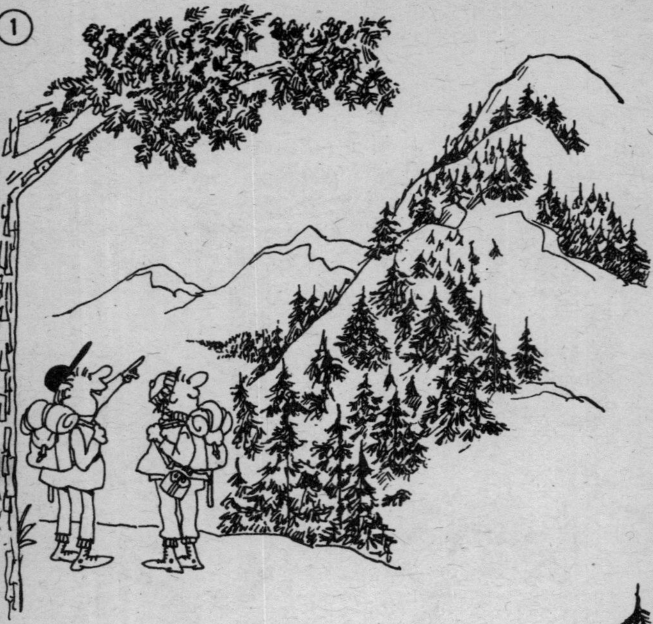

2

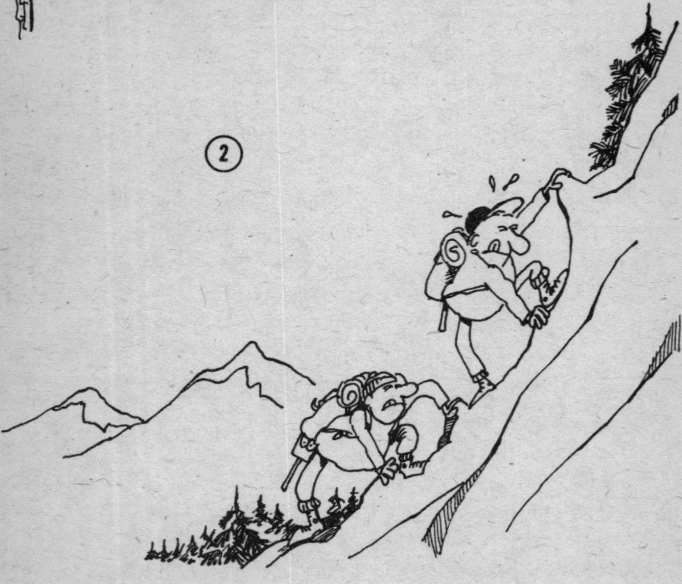

3

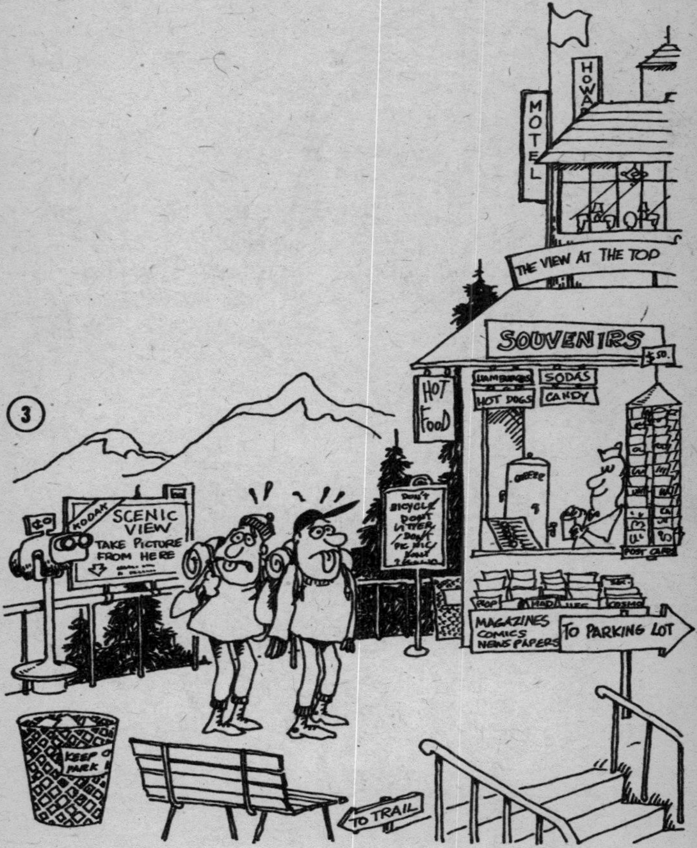

MOTEL
THE VIEW AT THE TOP
SOUVENIRS
HOT FOOD
HAMBURGERS
SODAS
HOT DOGS
CANDY
KODAK
SCENIC VIEW
TAKE PICTURE FROM HERE
DON'T BICYCLE
DON'T LITTER
MAGAZINES
COMICS
NEWS PAPERS
TO PARKING LOT
POST CARDS
TO TRAIL

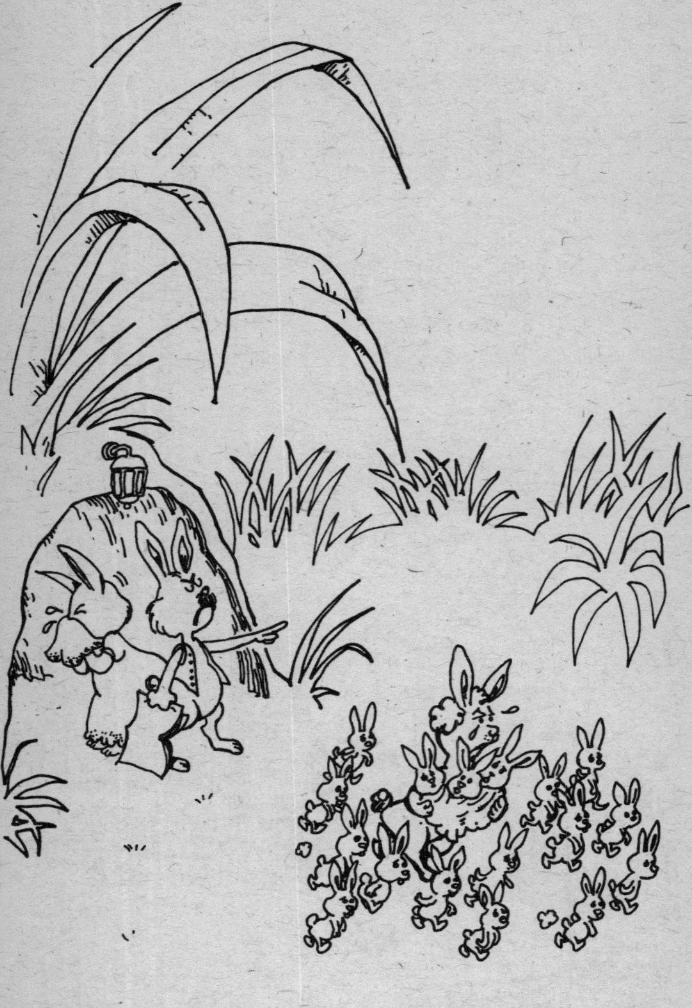

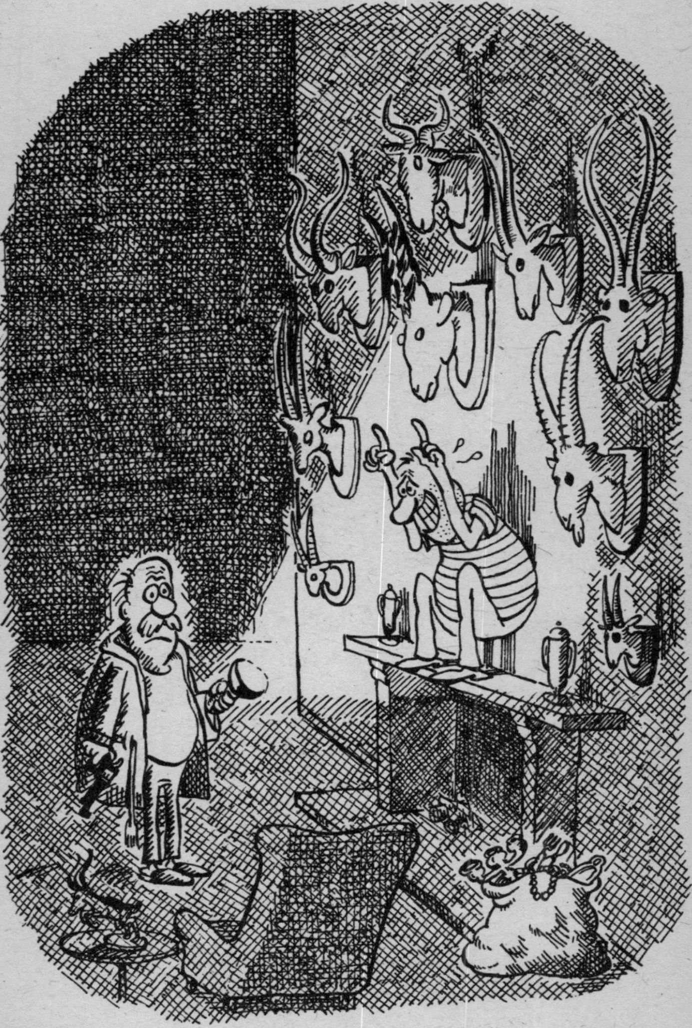

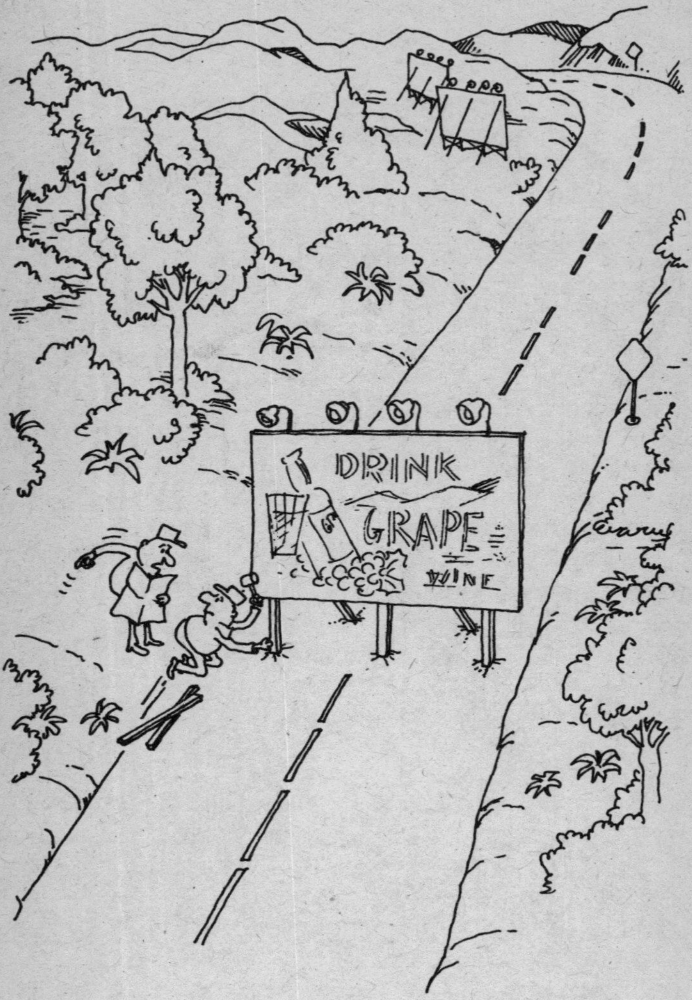
DRINK
GRAPE
WINE

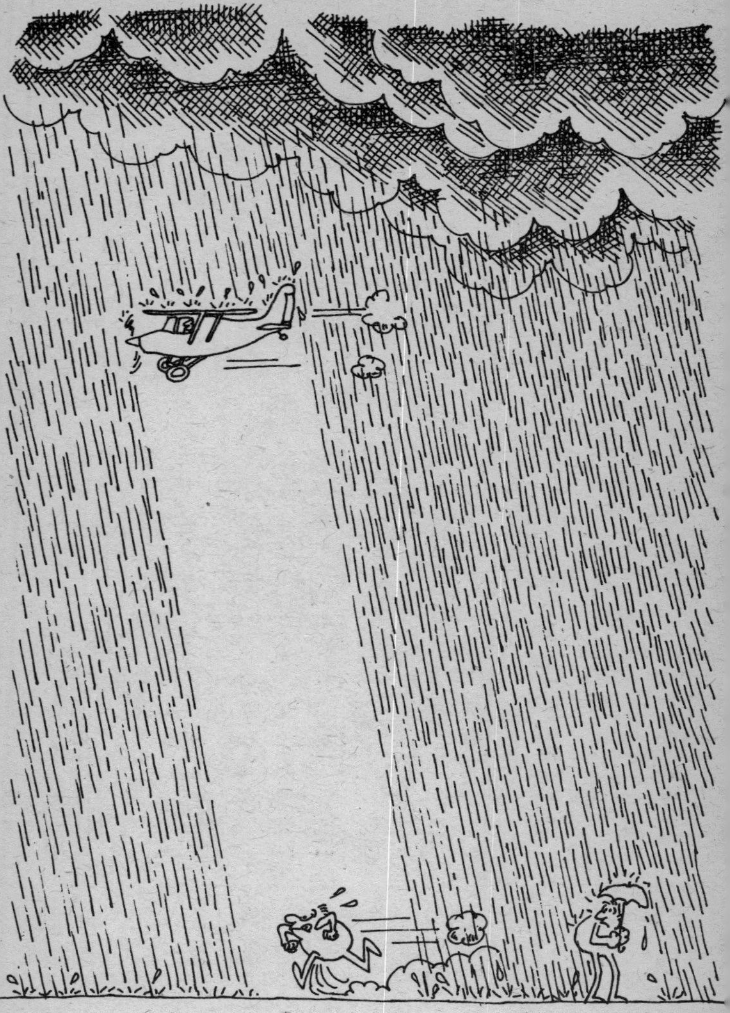

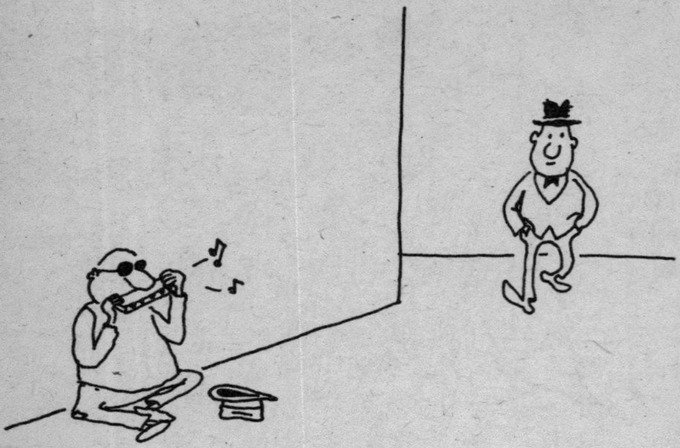

2

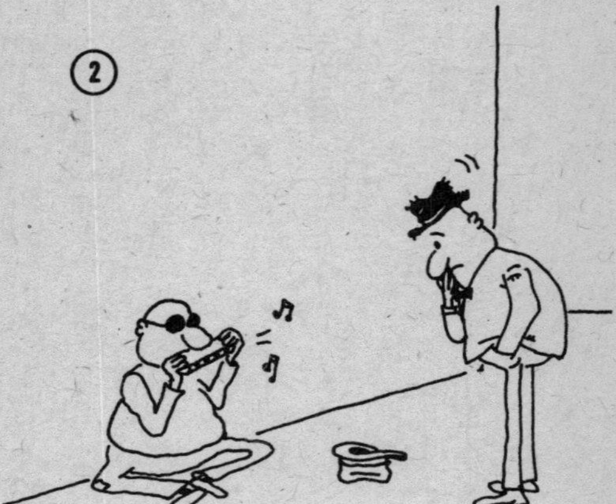

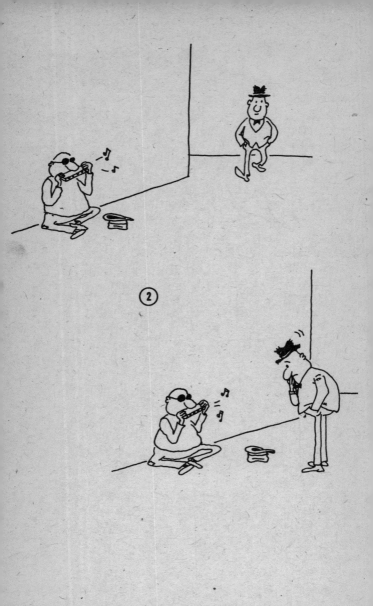

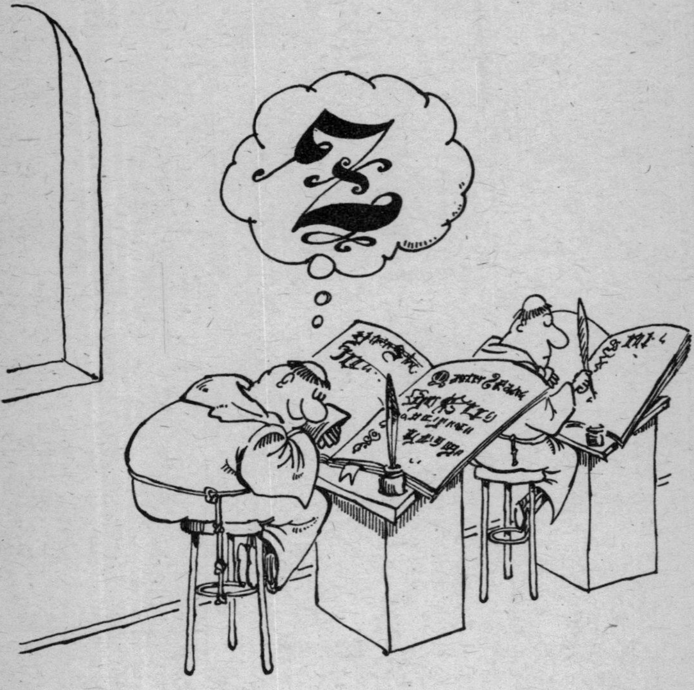
Z

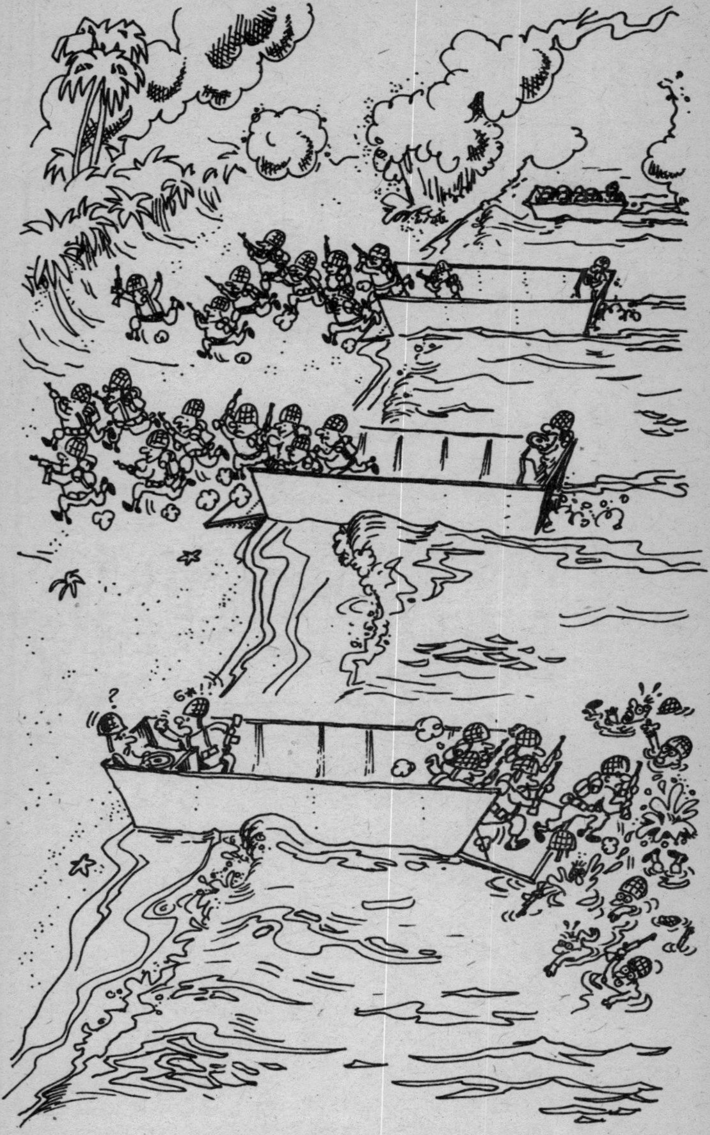

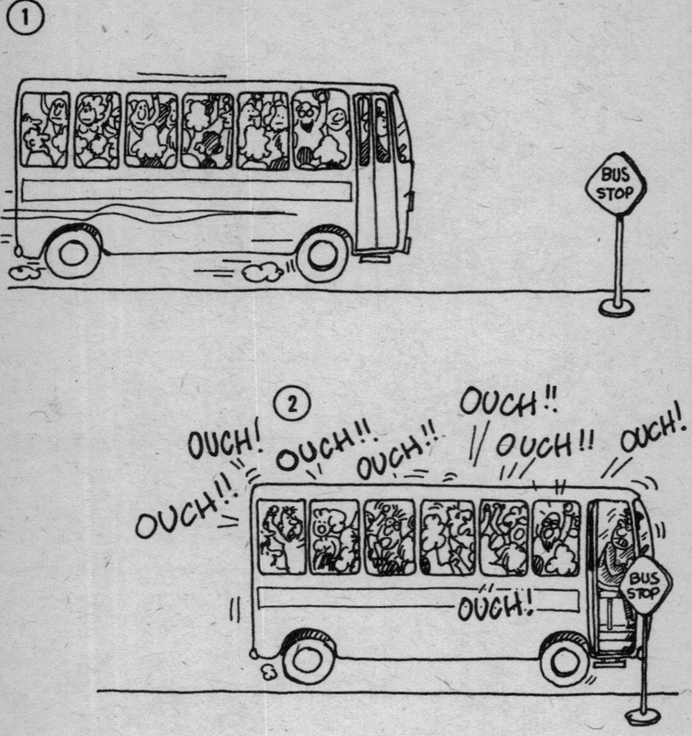
1
BUS STOP
2
OUCH!
OUCH!!
OUCH!!
OUCH!!
OUCH!!
OUCH!!
OUCH!
OUCH!
BUS STOP

3

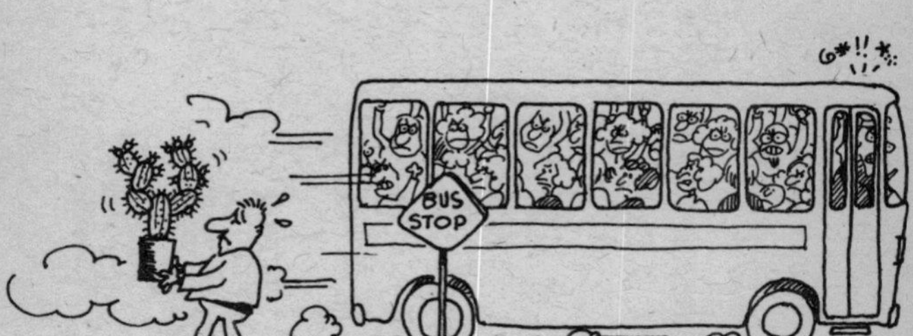
BUS
STOP

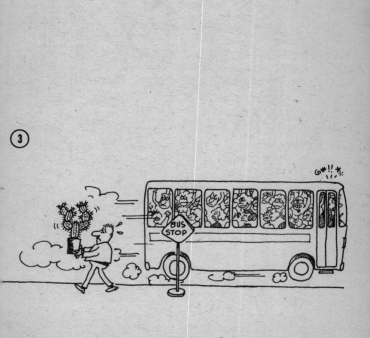

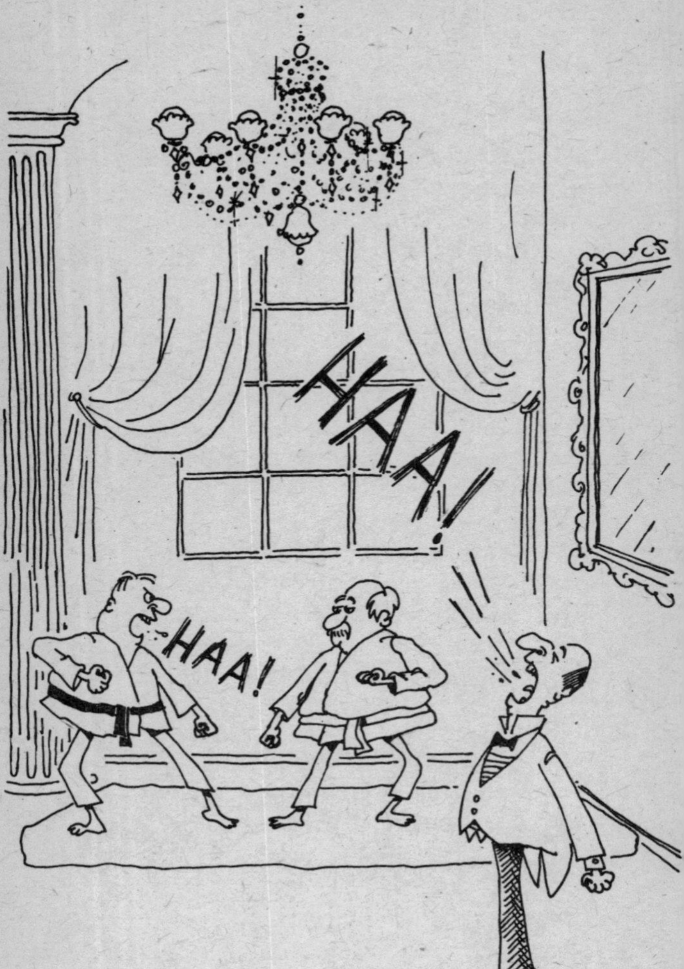

HAA!
HAA!

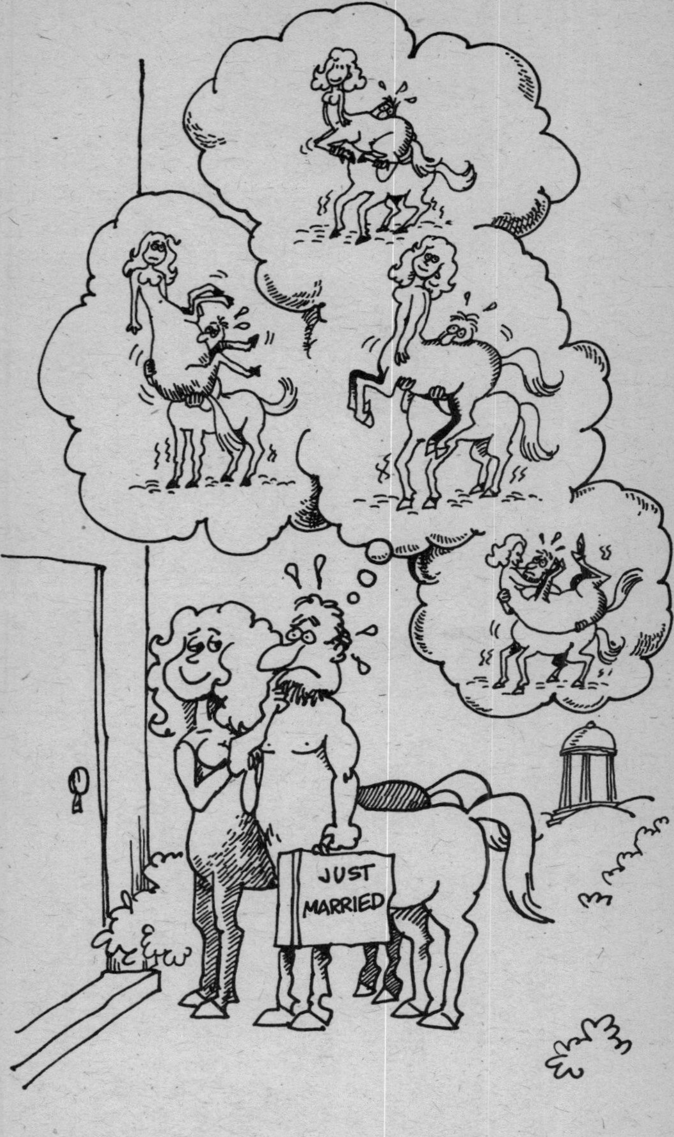
JUST MARRIED

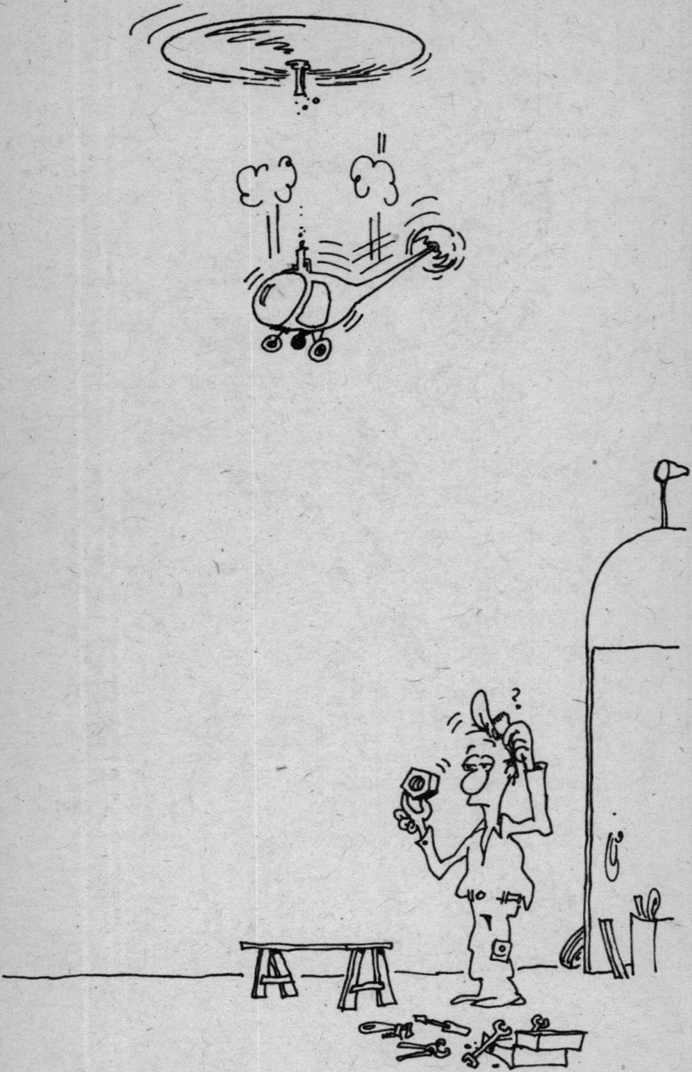

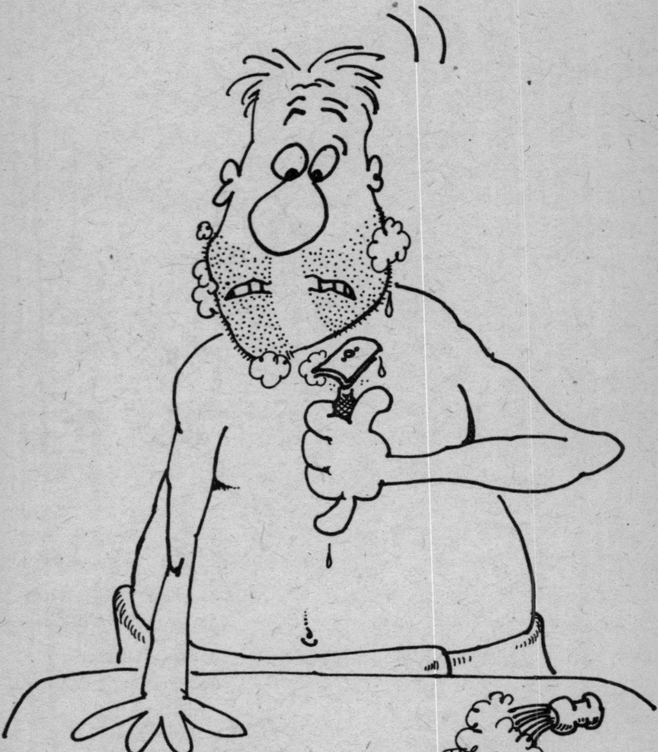

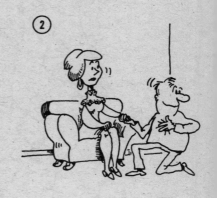

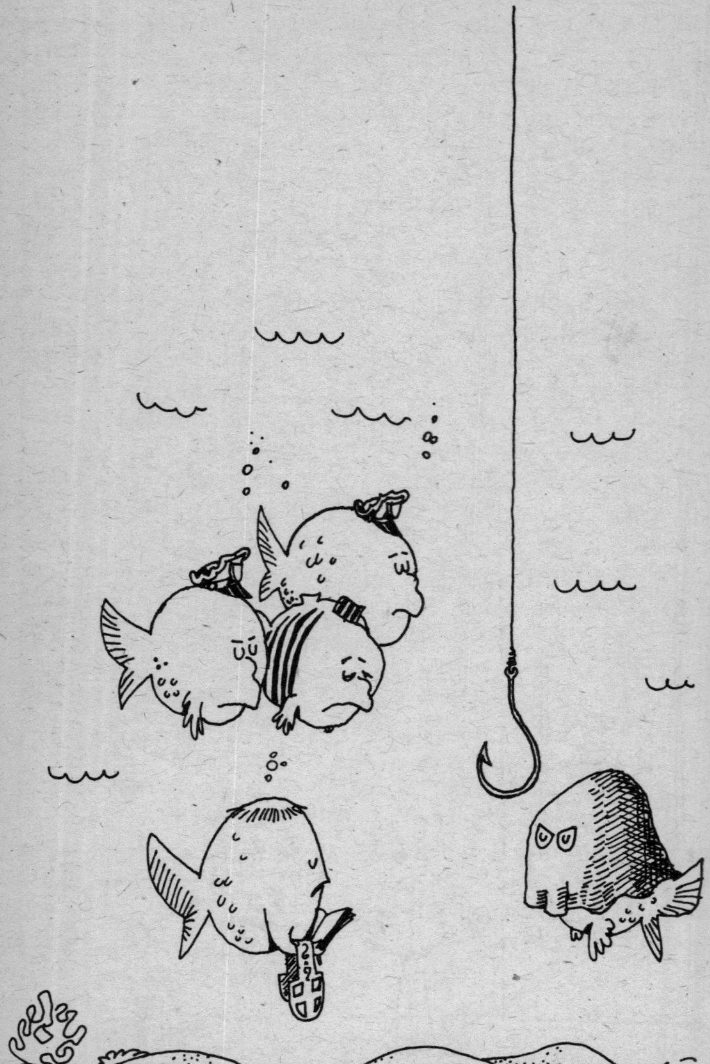

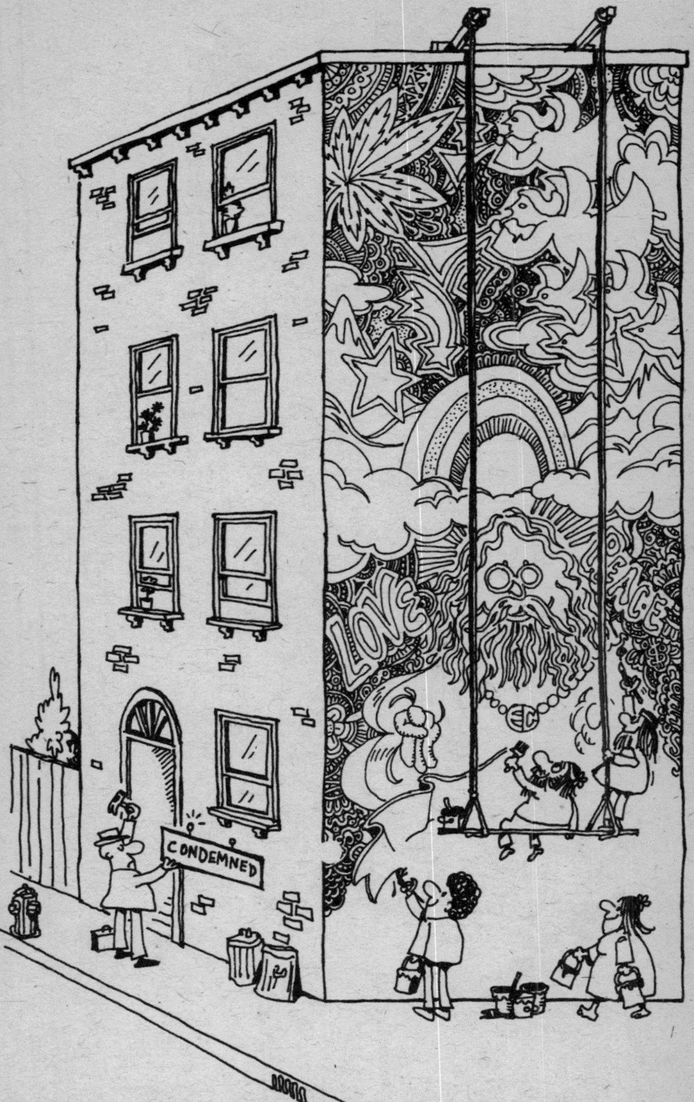
CONDEMNED
LOVE
PEACE

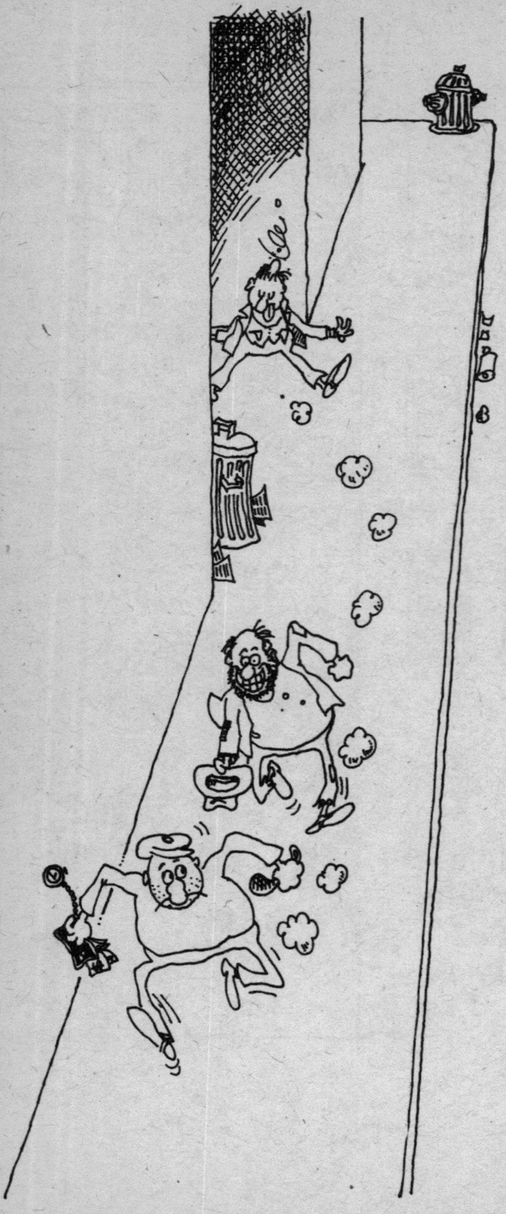

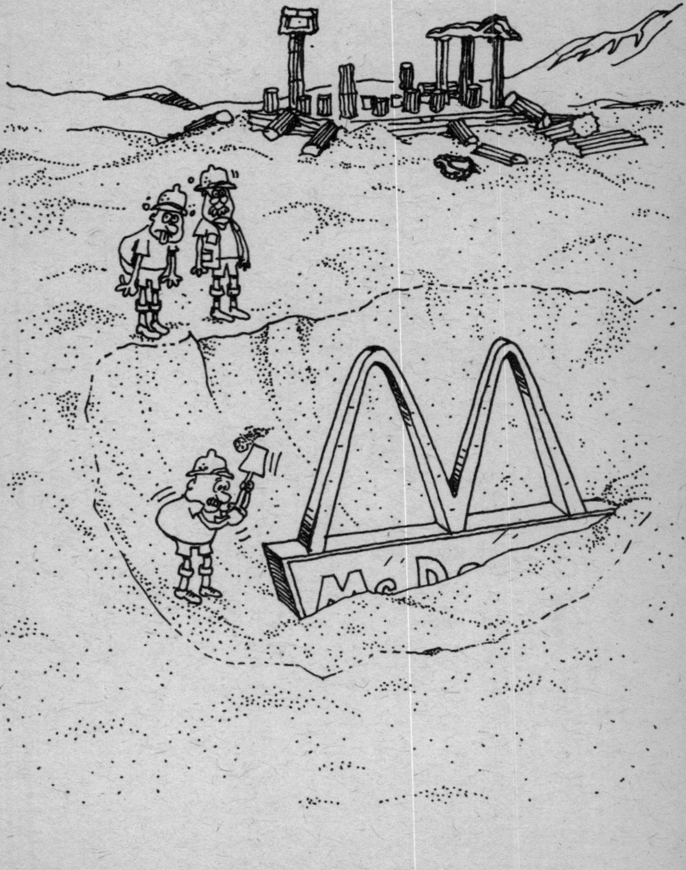
McD

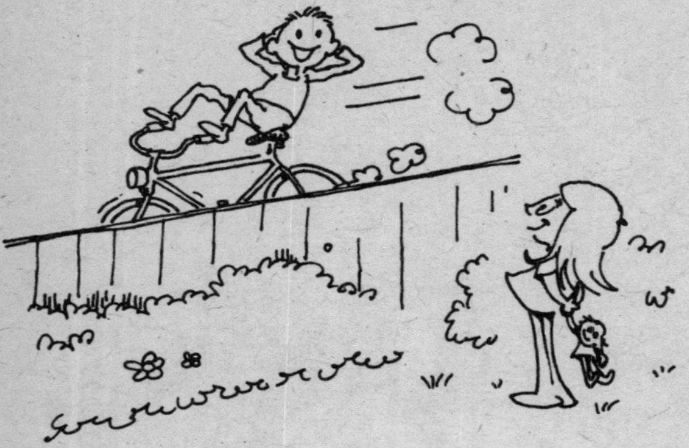

2

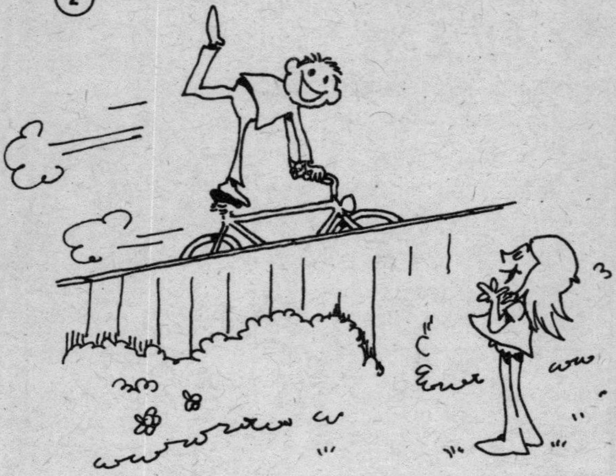

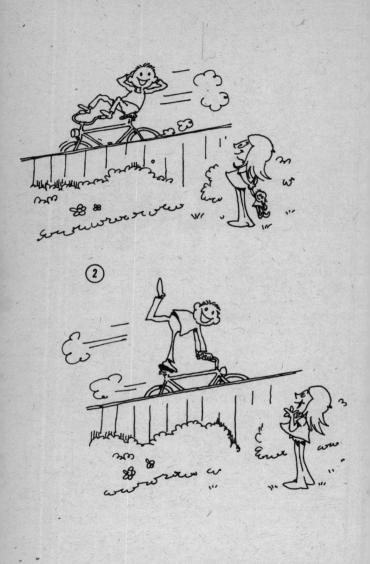

③

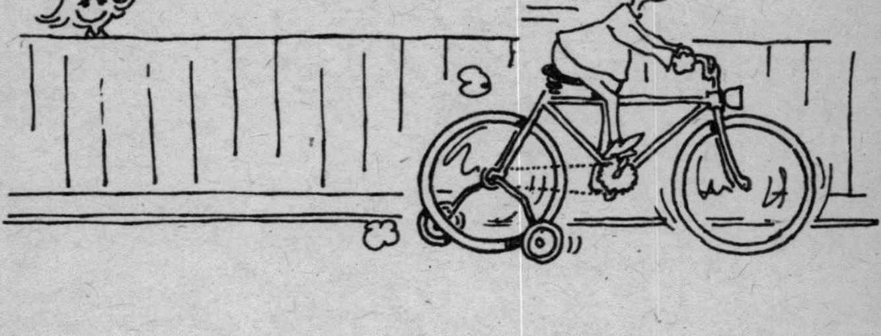

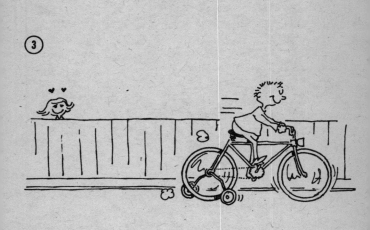

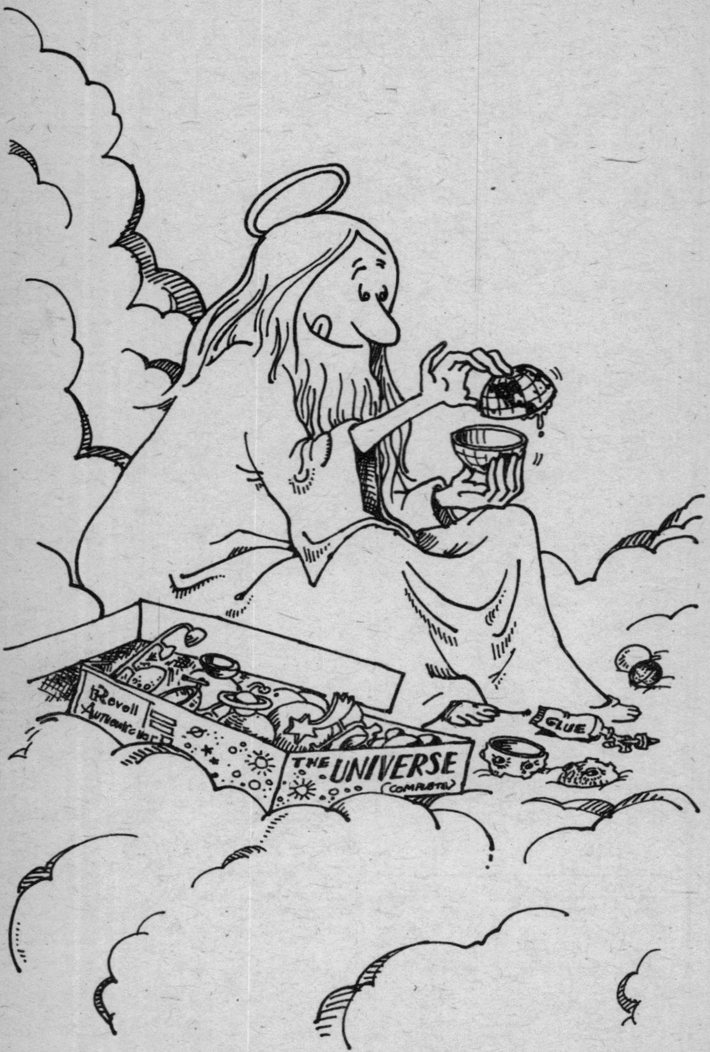
Revell
THE UNIVERSE
GLUE

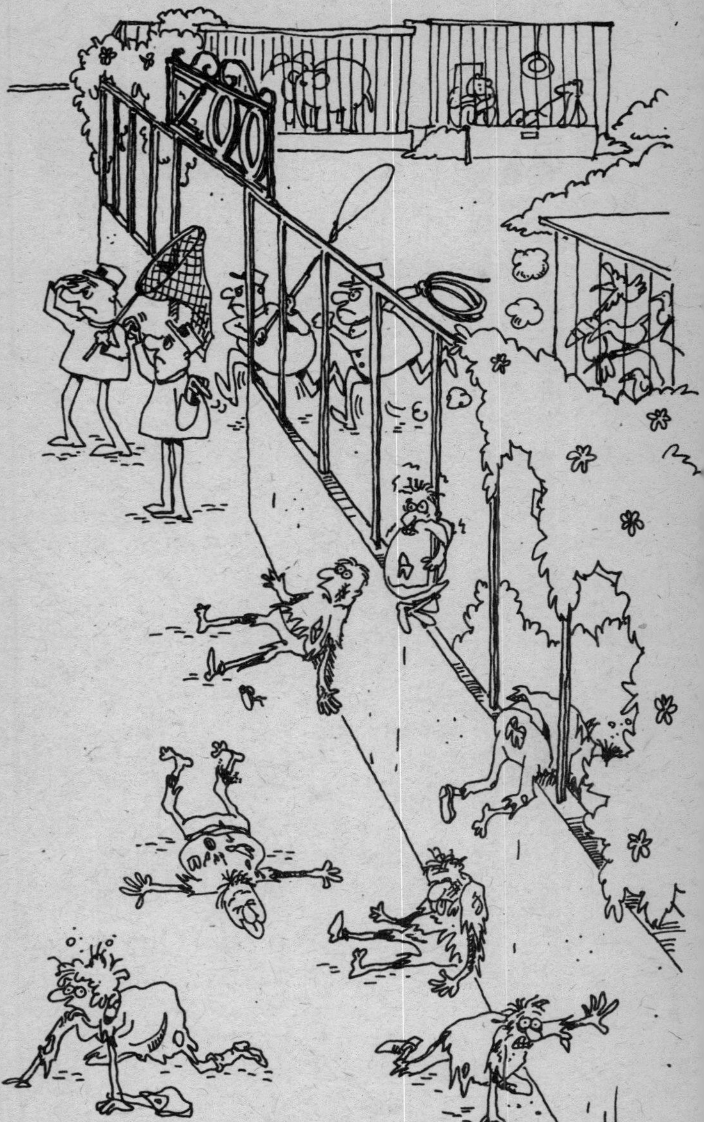
ZOO

1

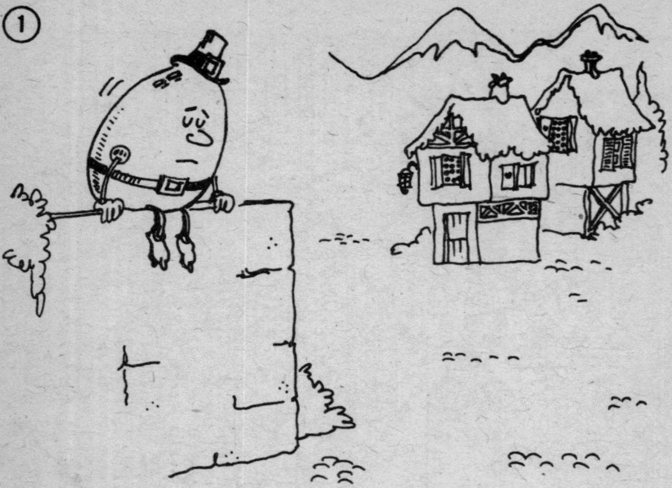

2

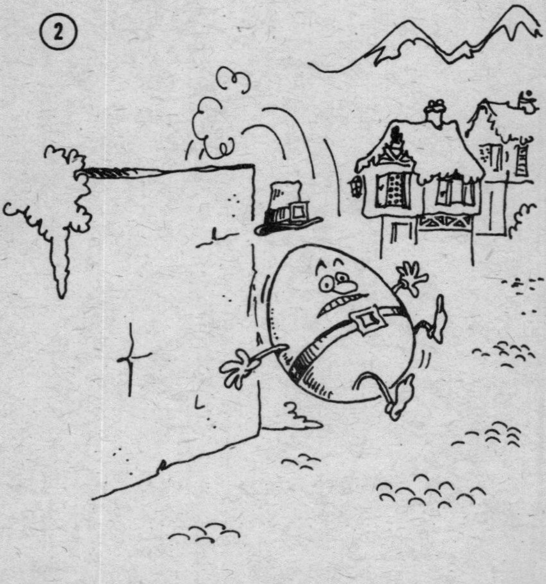

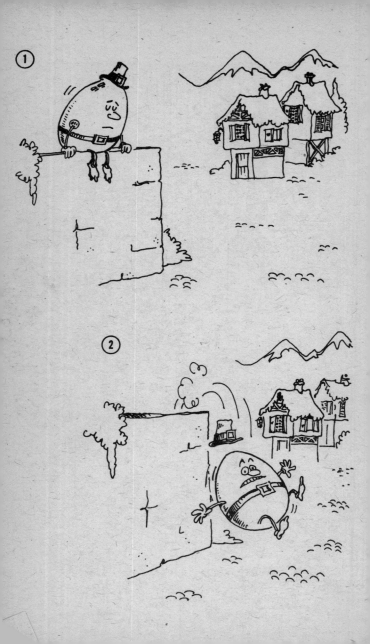

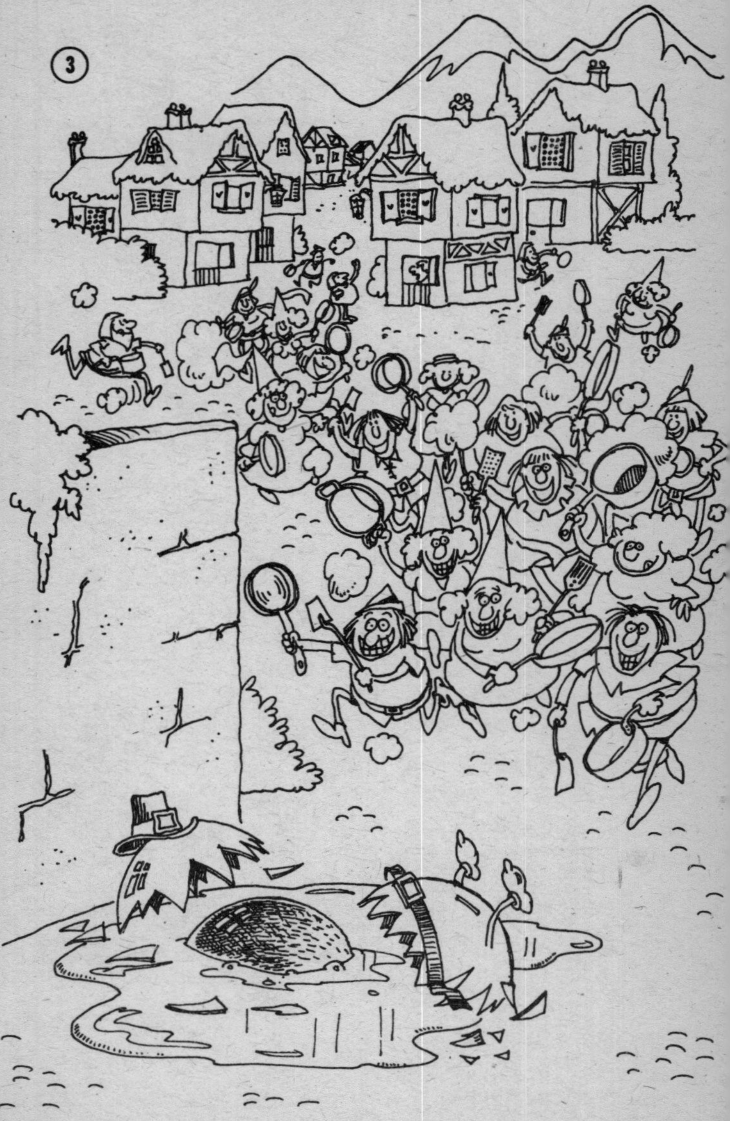
3

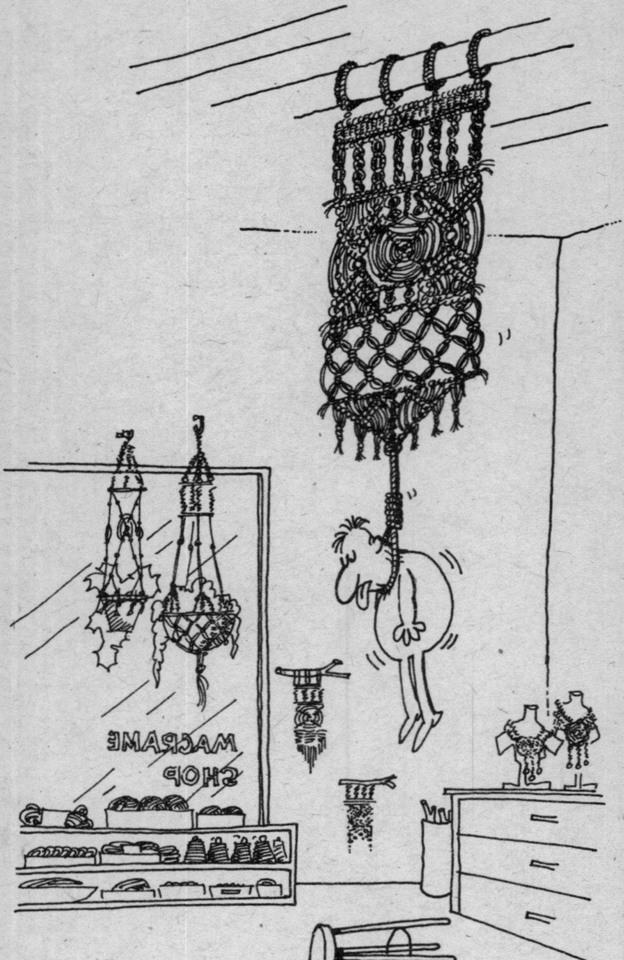
MACRAME
SHOP

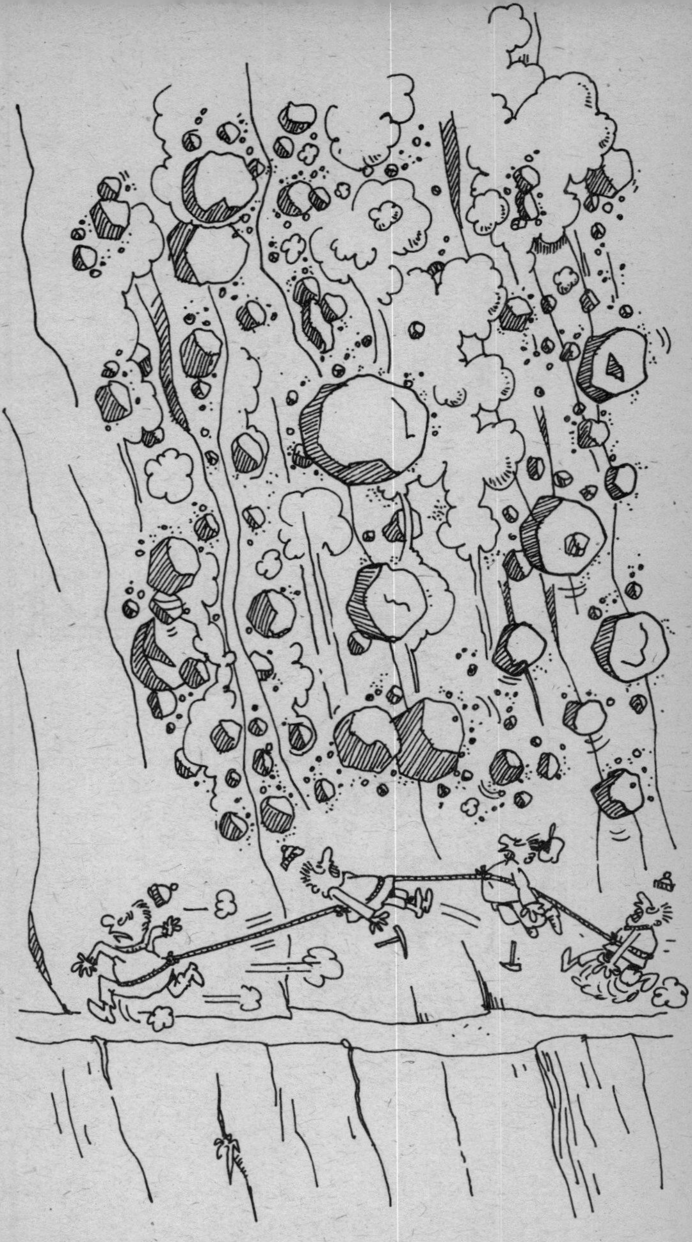

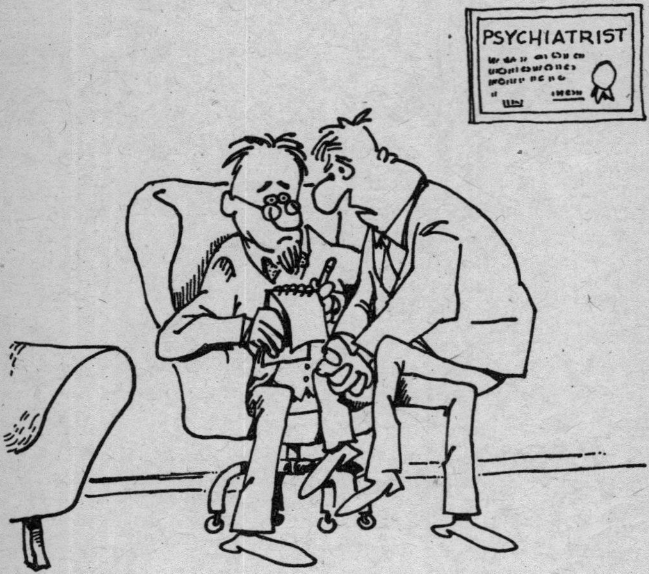
PSYCHIATRIST

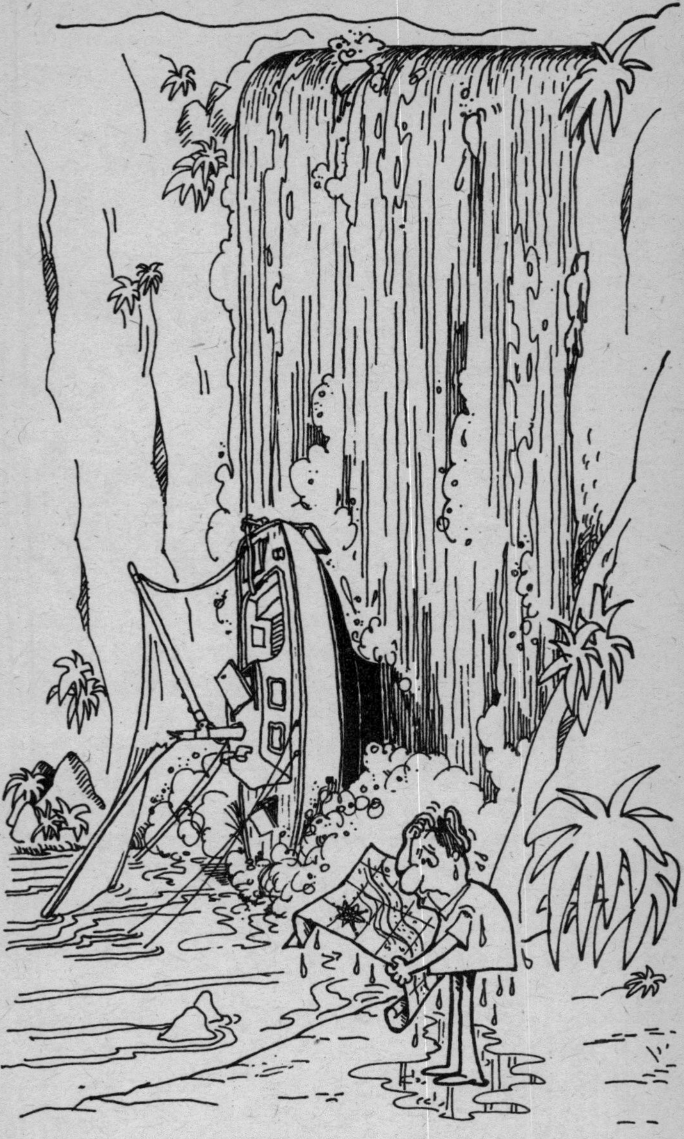

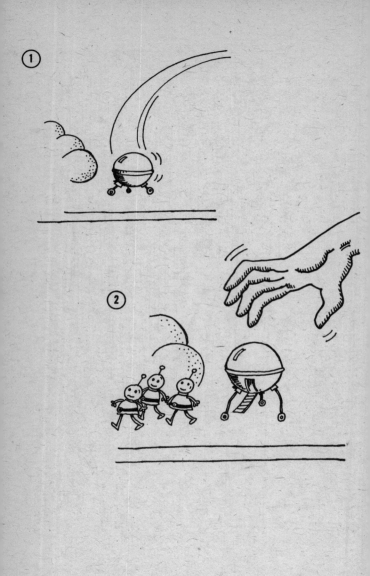

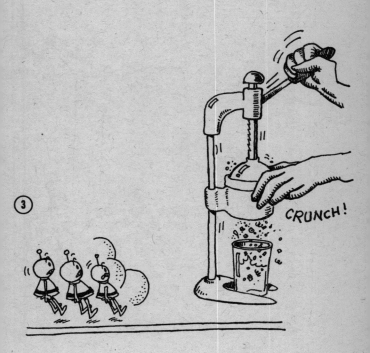

CRUNCH!

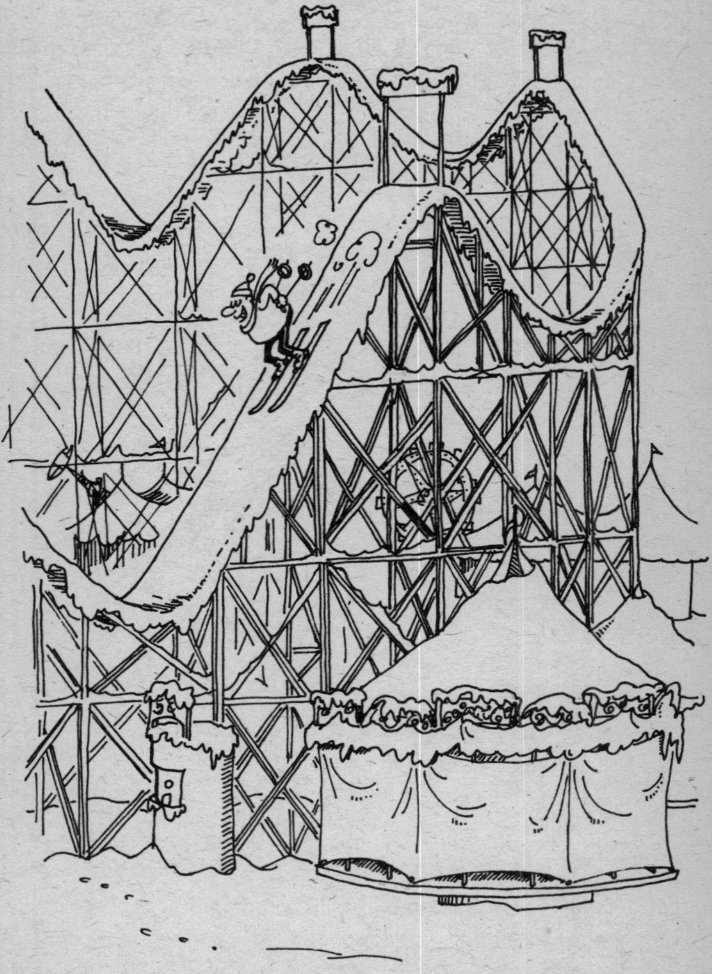

①

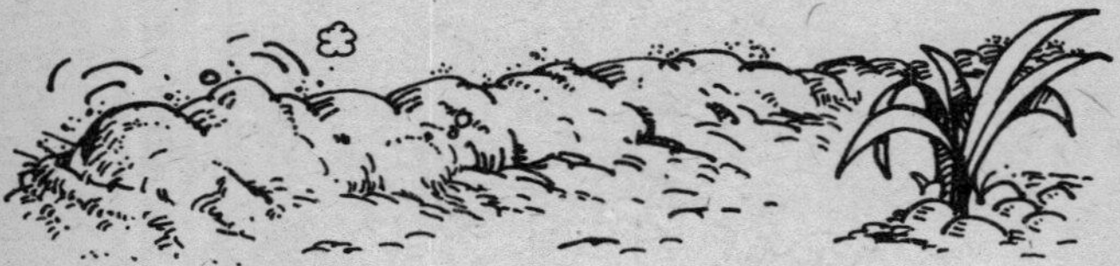

②

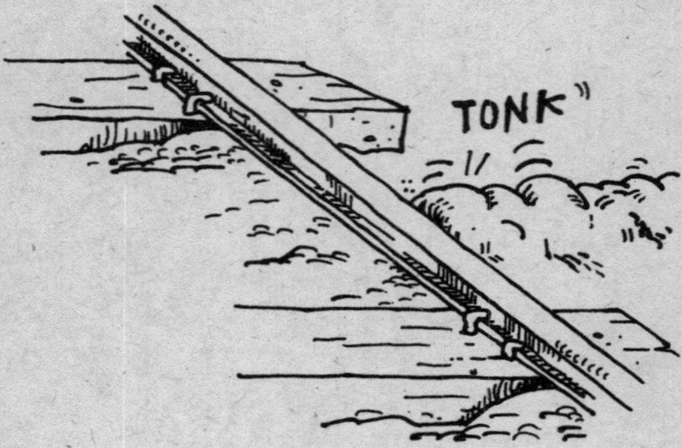
TONK"

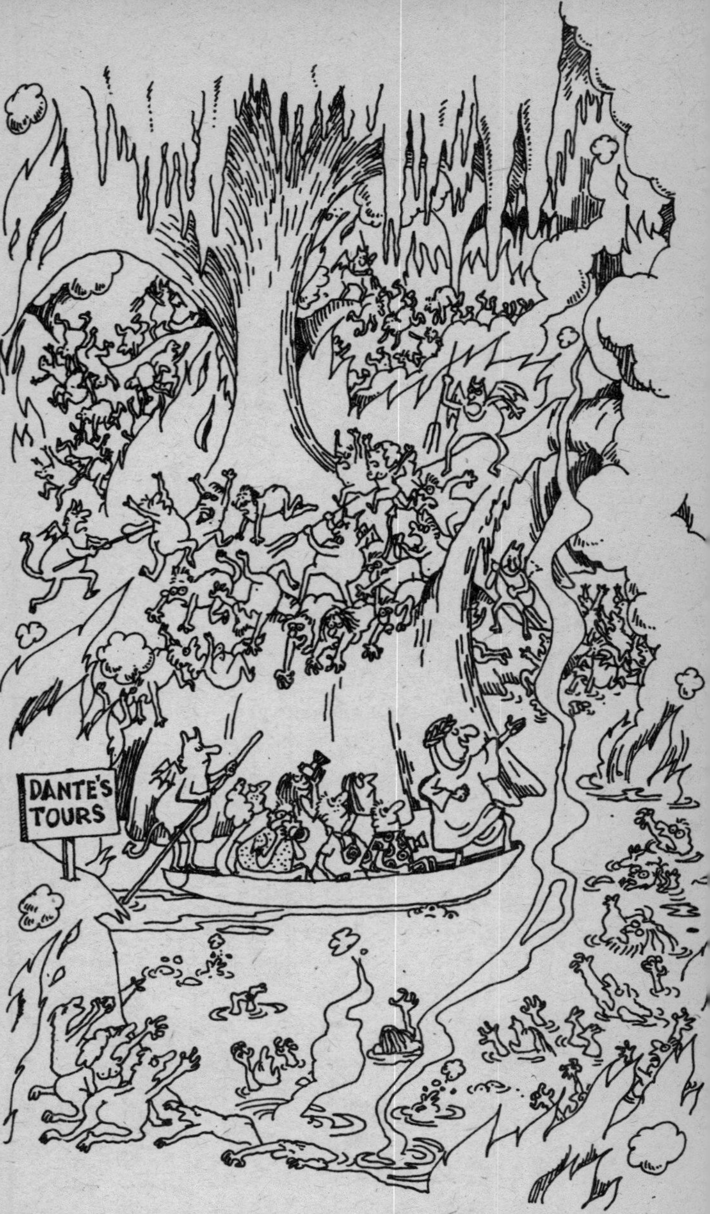
DANTE'S
TOURS

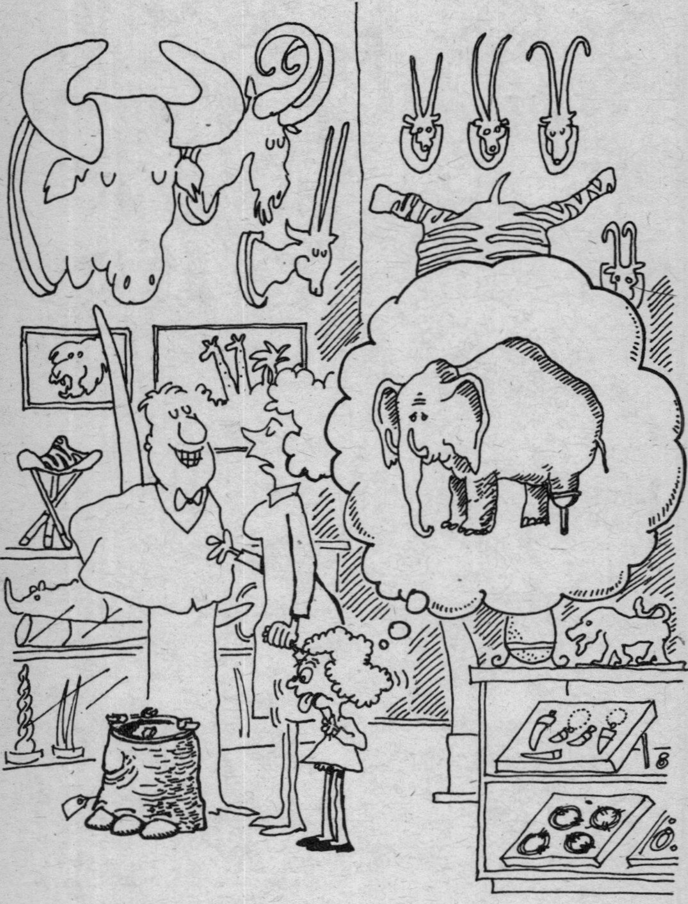

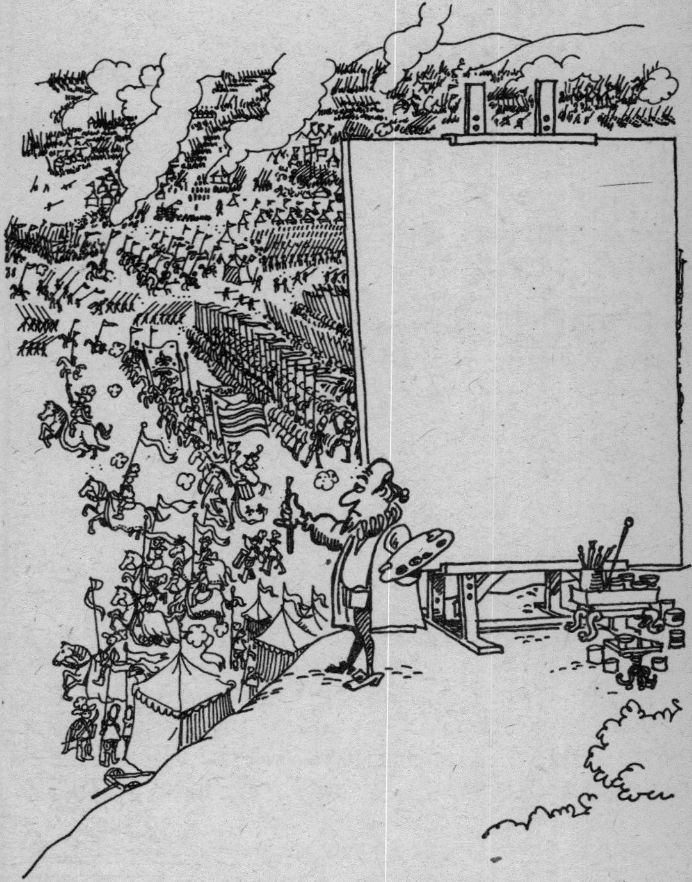

1

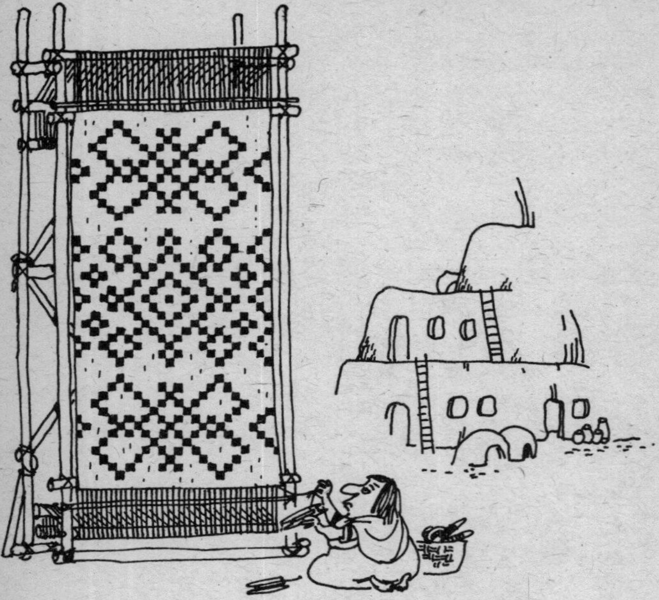

2

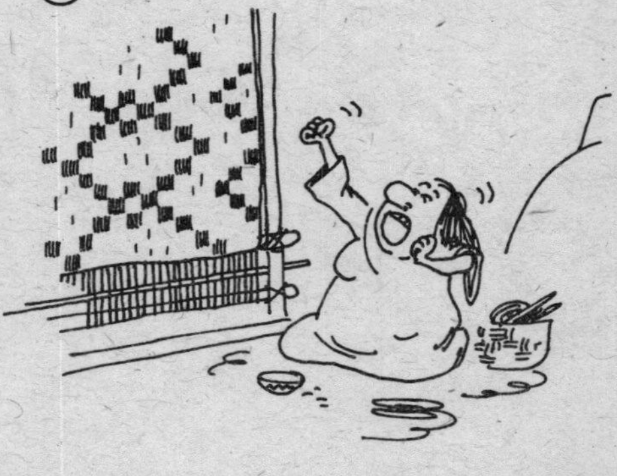

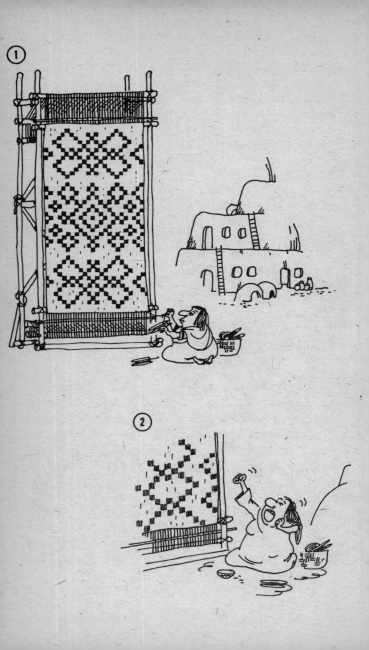

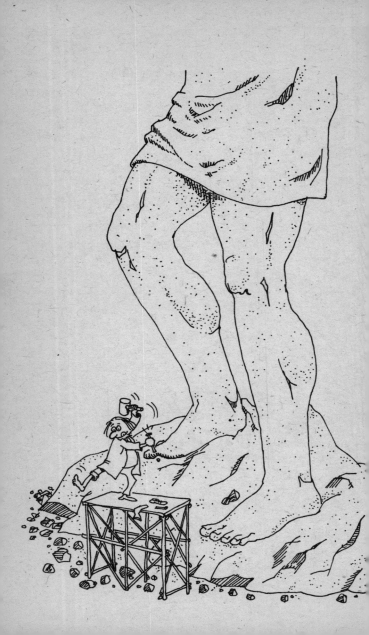

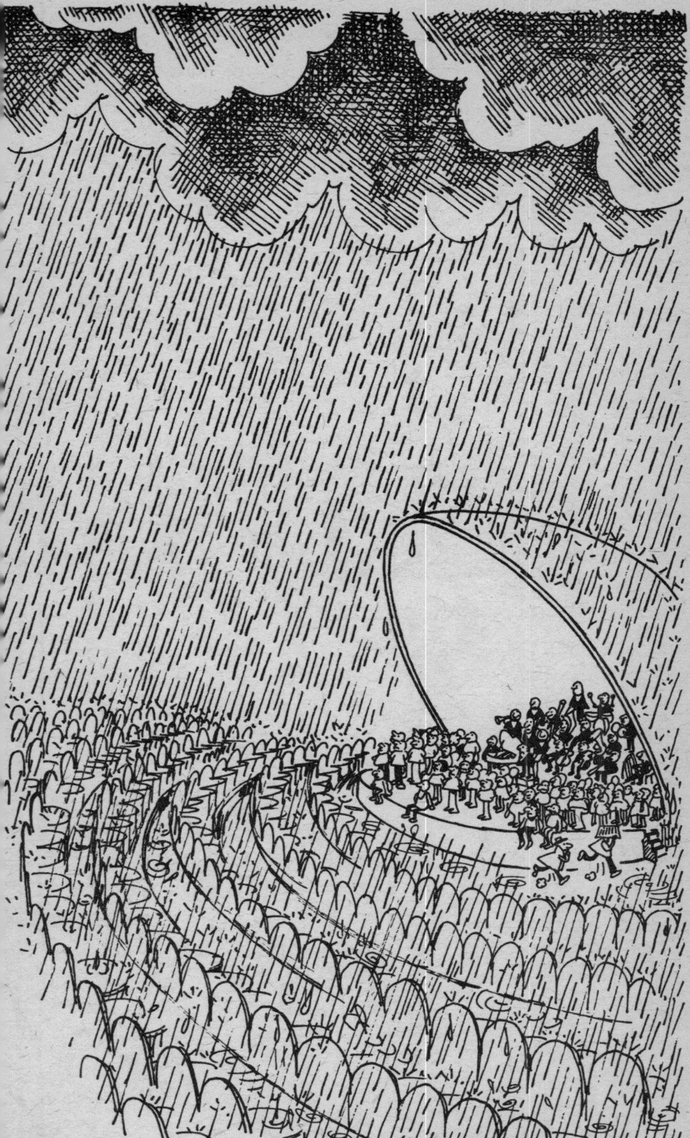

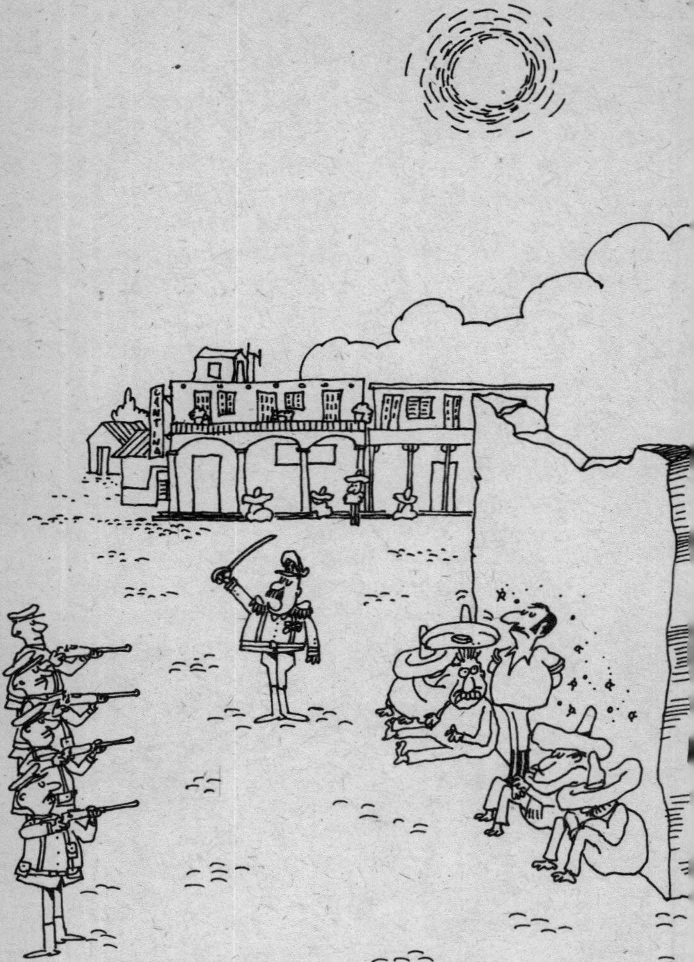
CANTINA

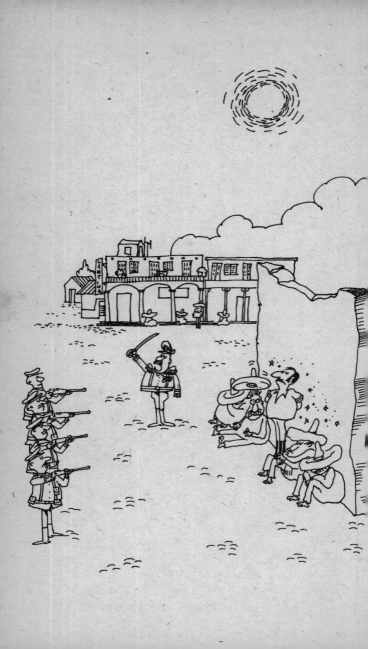

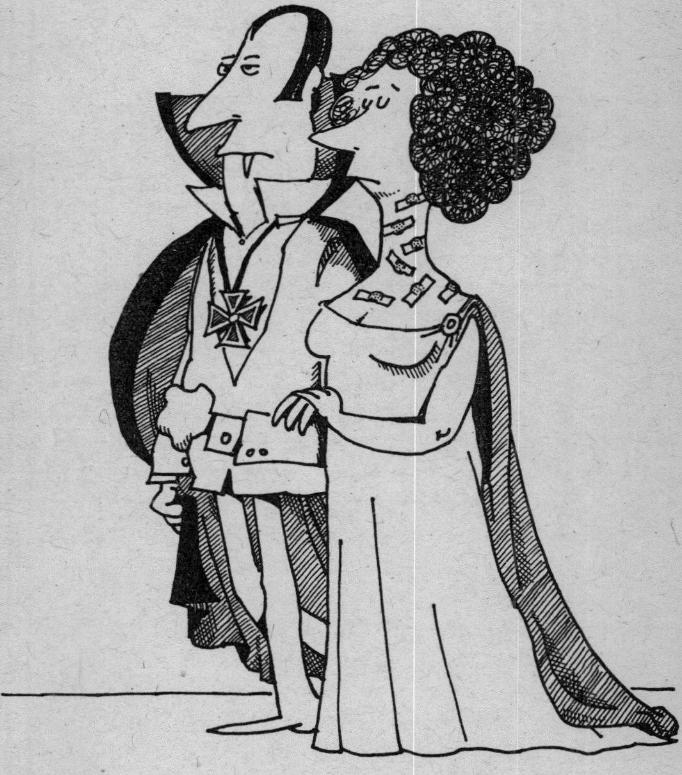

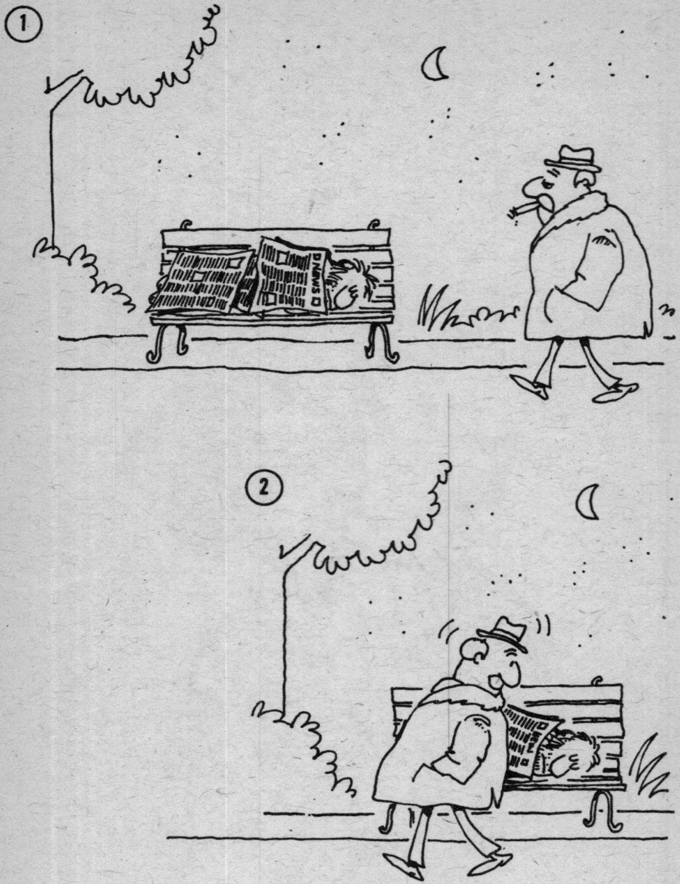
1
NEWS
2

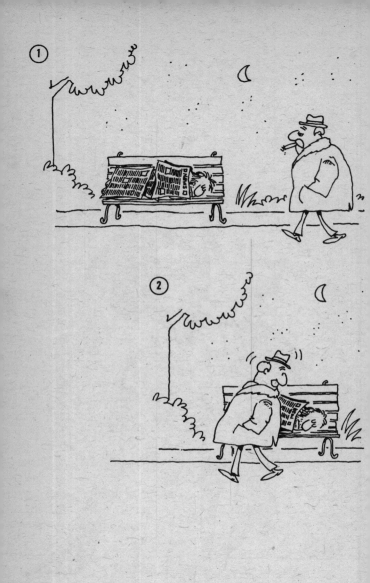

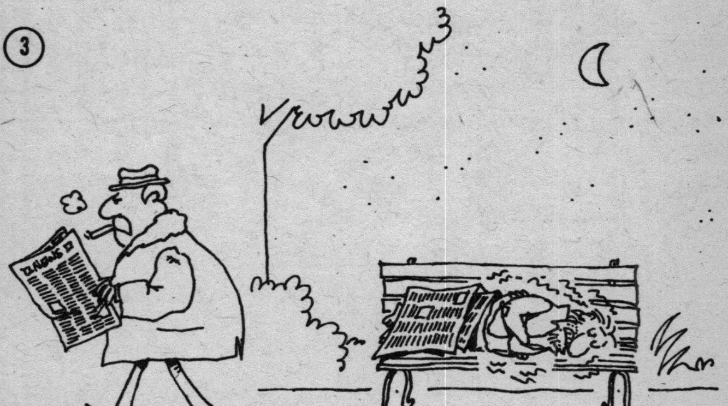
3
NEWS

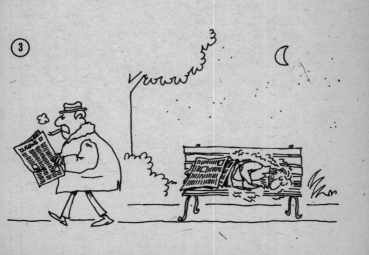

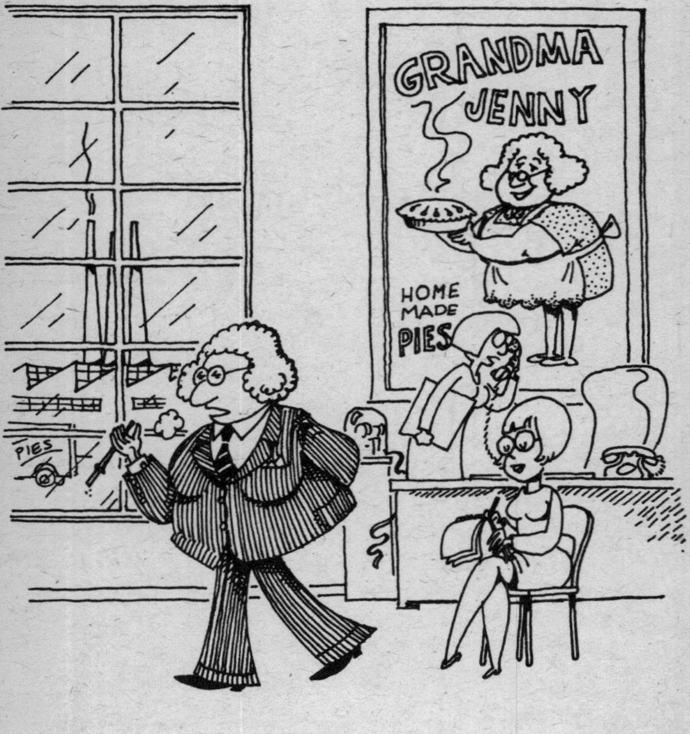

GRANDMA
JENNY
HOME
MADE
PIES
PIES

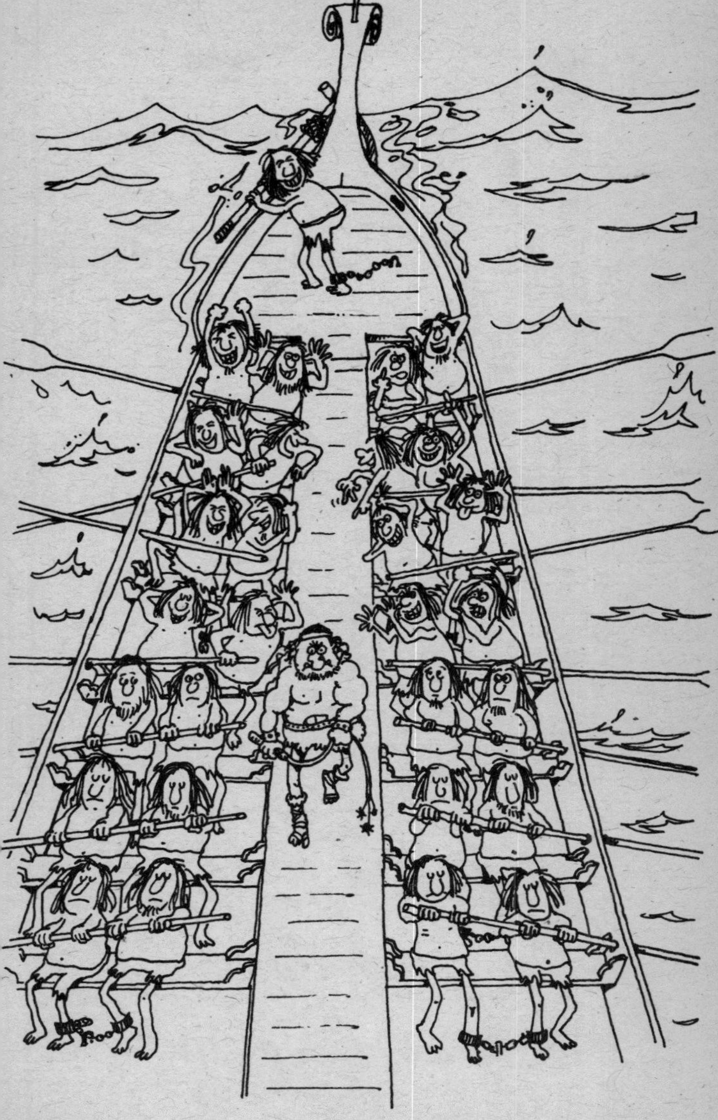

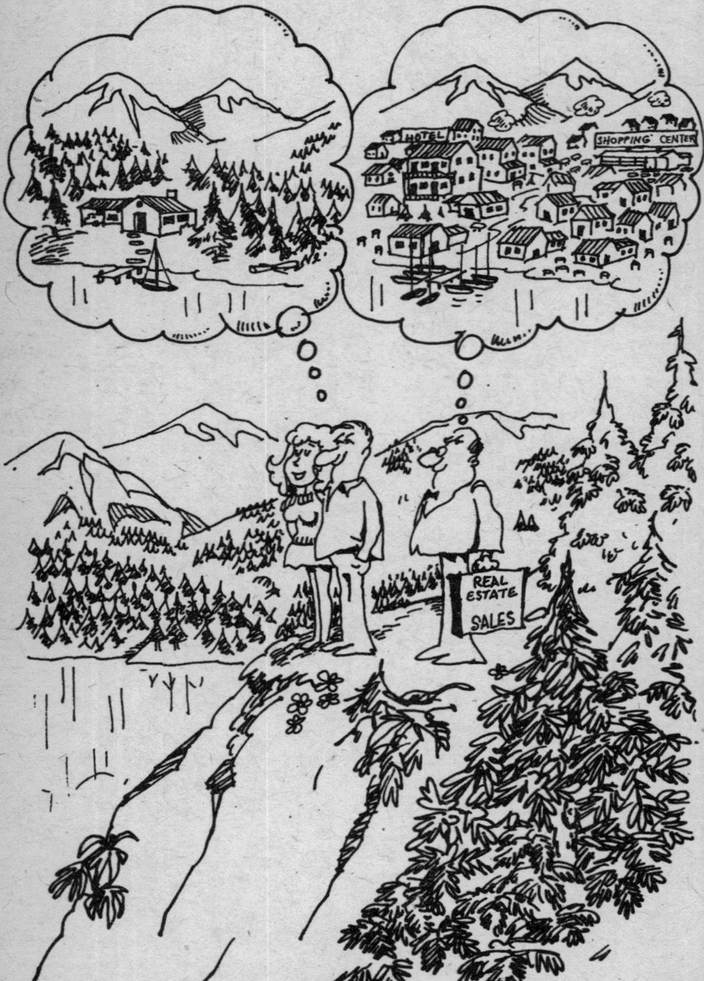
HOTEL
SHOPPING CENTER
REAL ESTATE
SALES

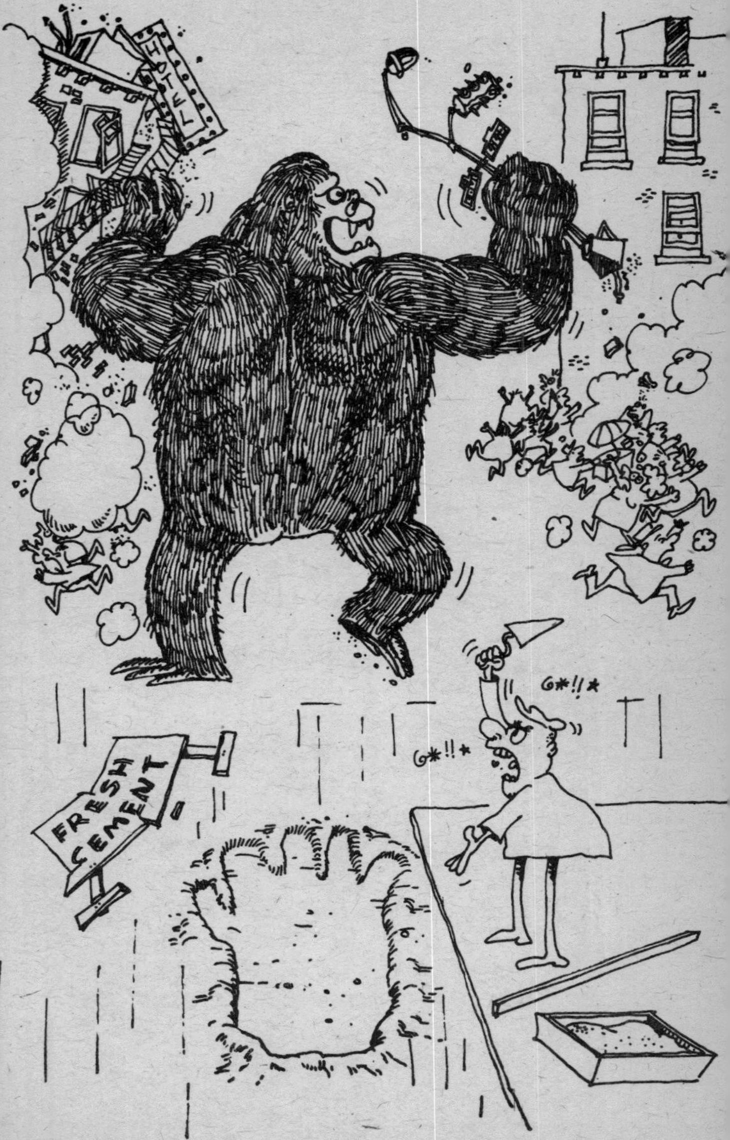
HOTEL
G*!!*
G*!!*
FRESH CEMENT

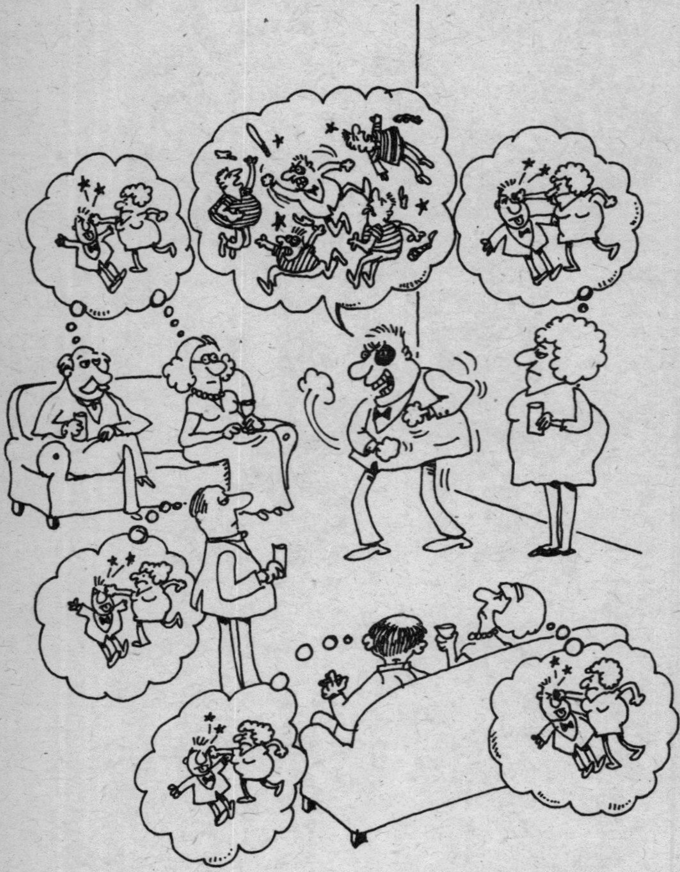

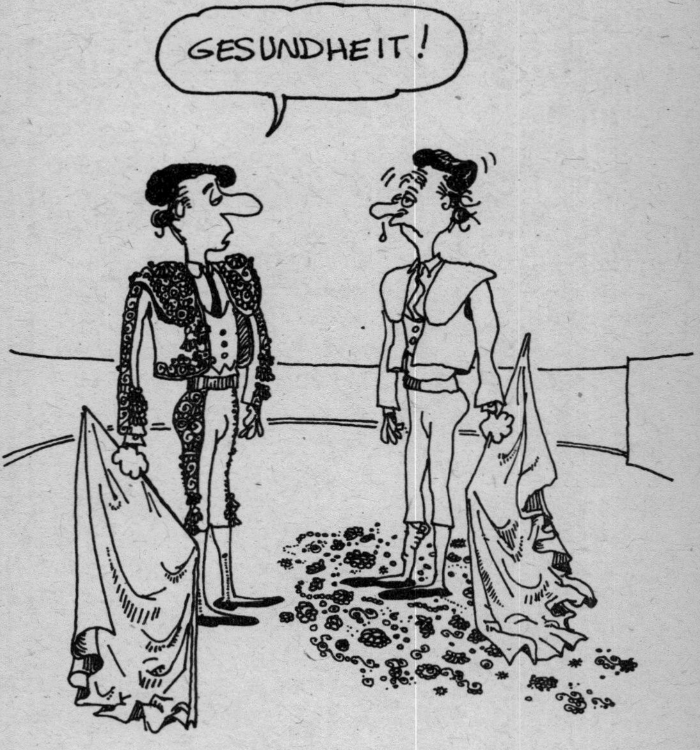
GESUNDHEIT!

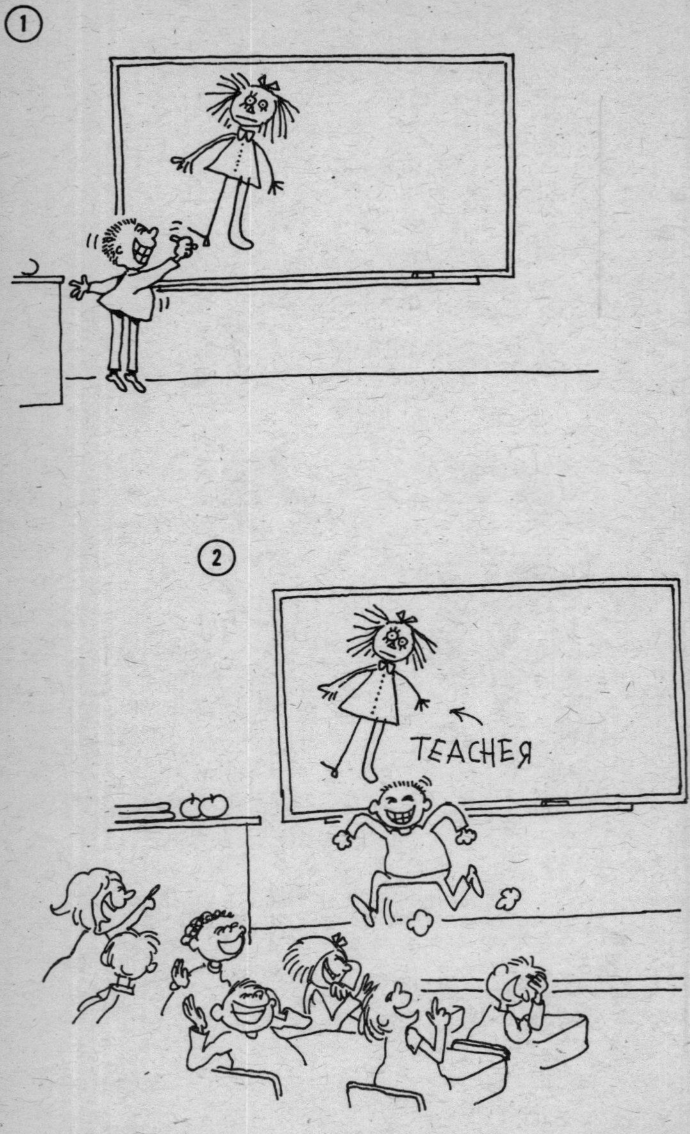
1
2
TEACHEЯ

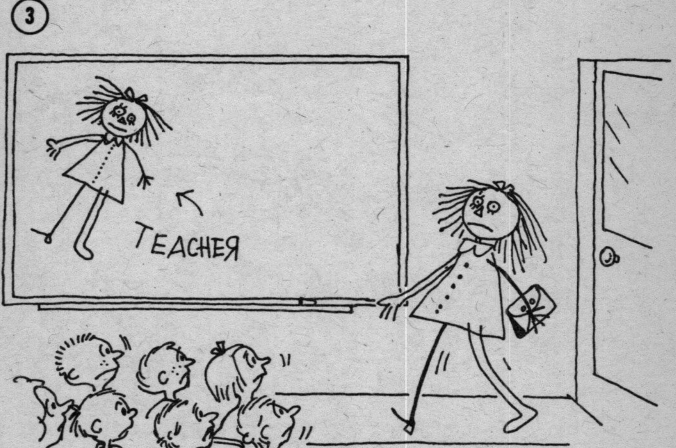
3
TEACHER

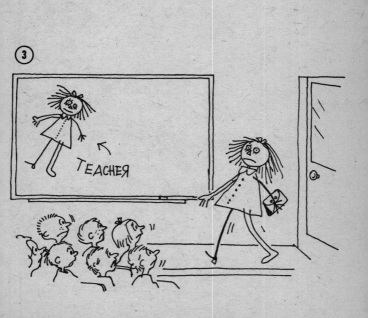

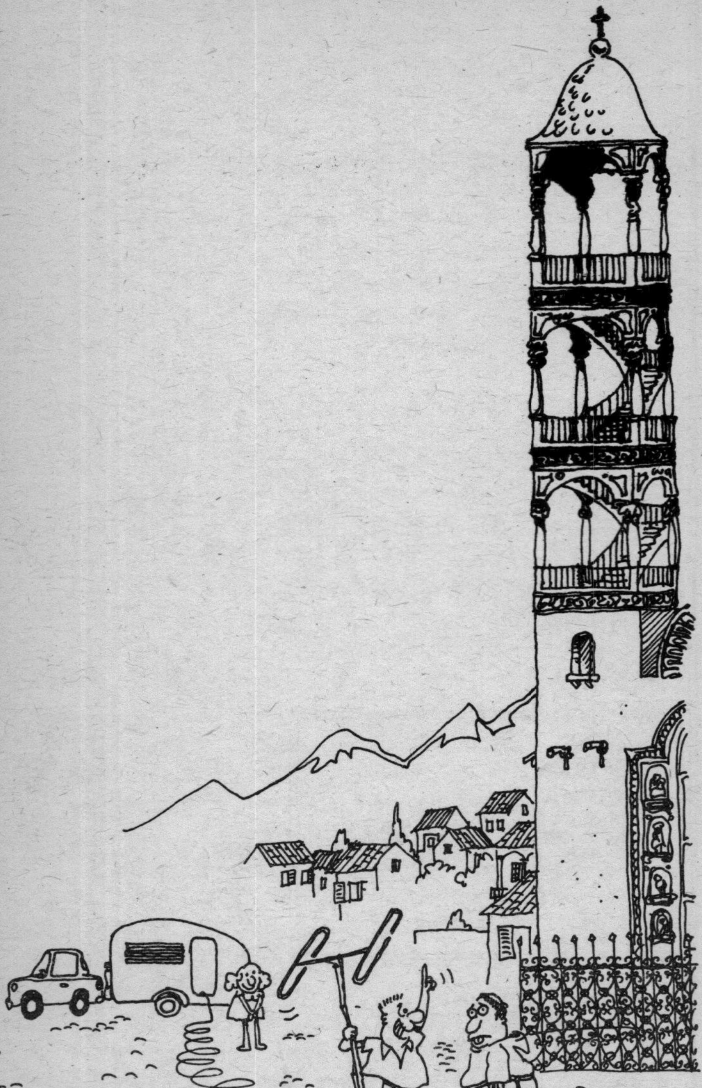

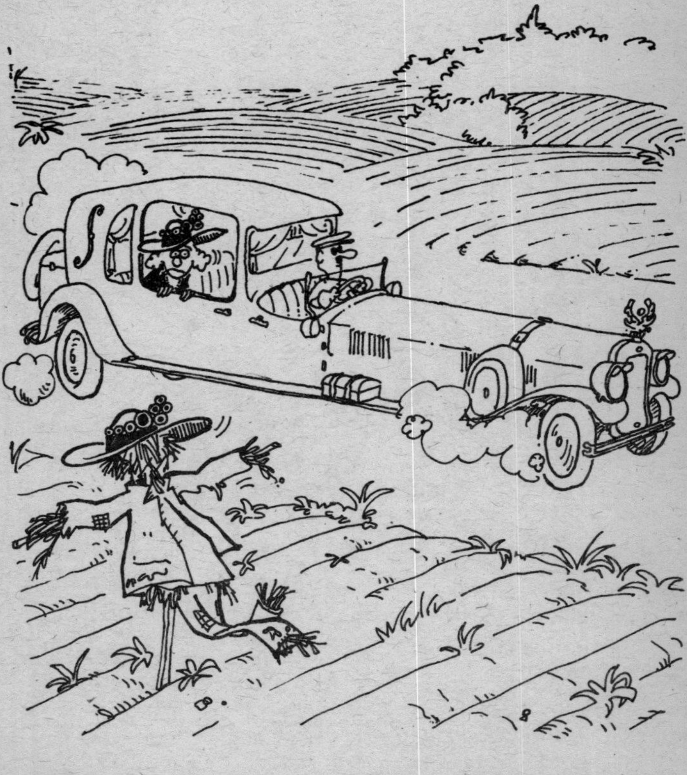

1

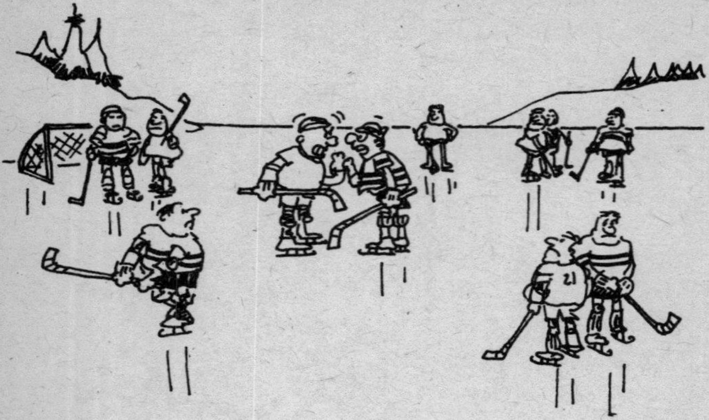
21

2

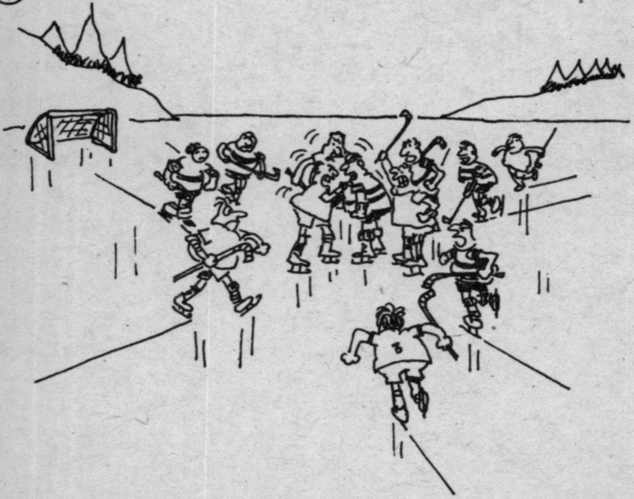

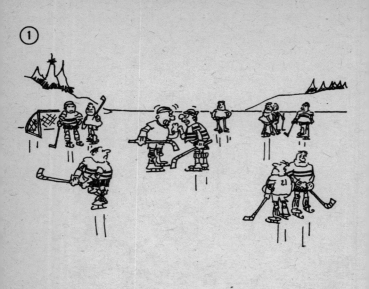

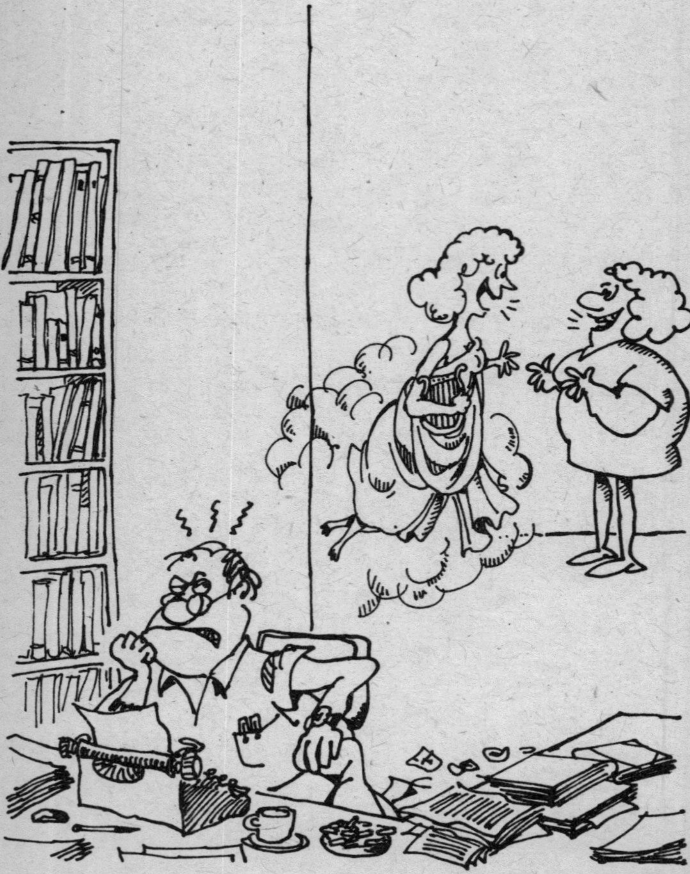

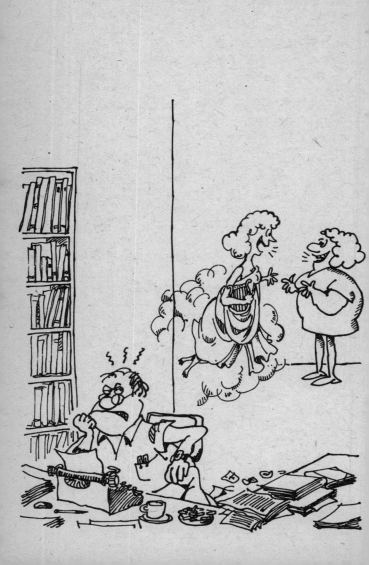

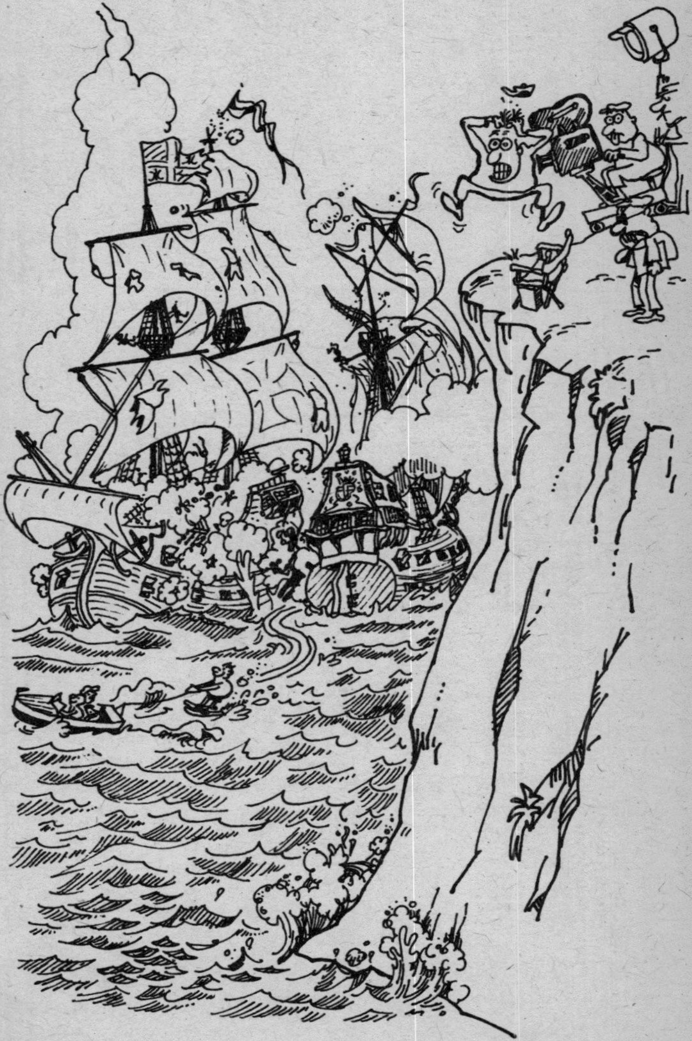

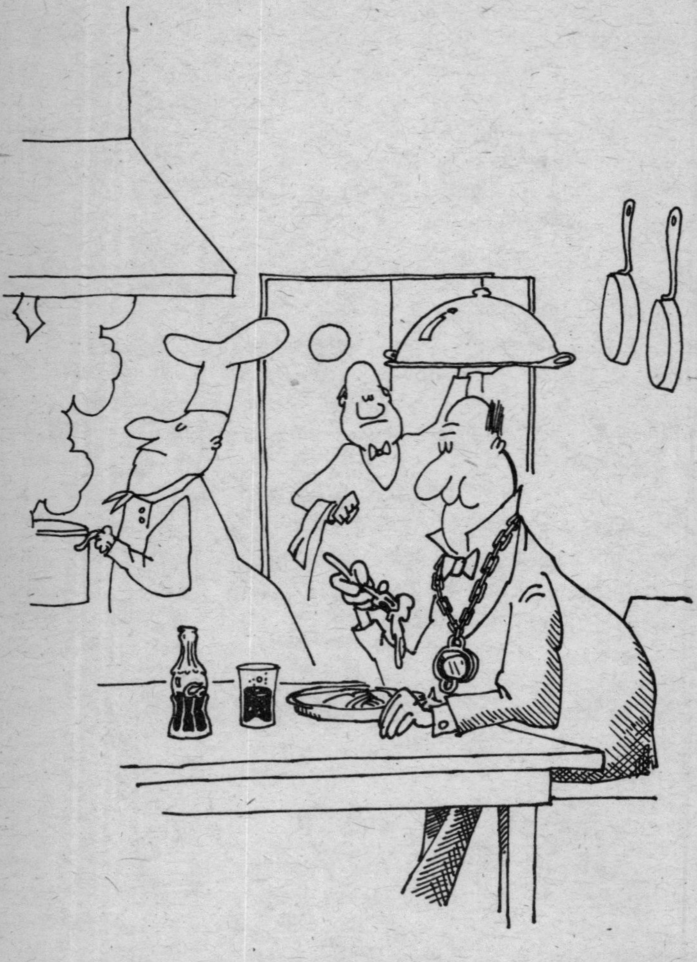

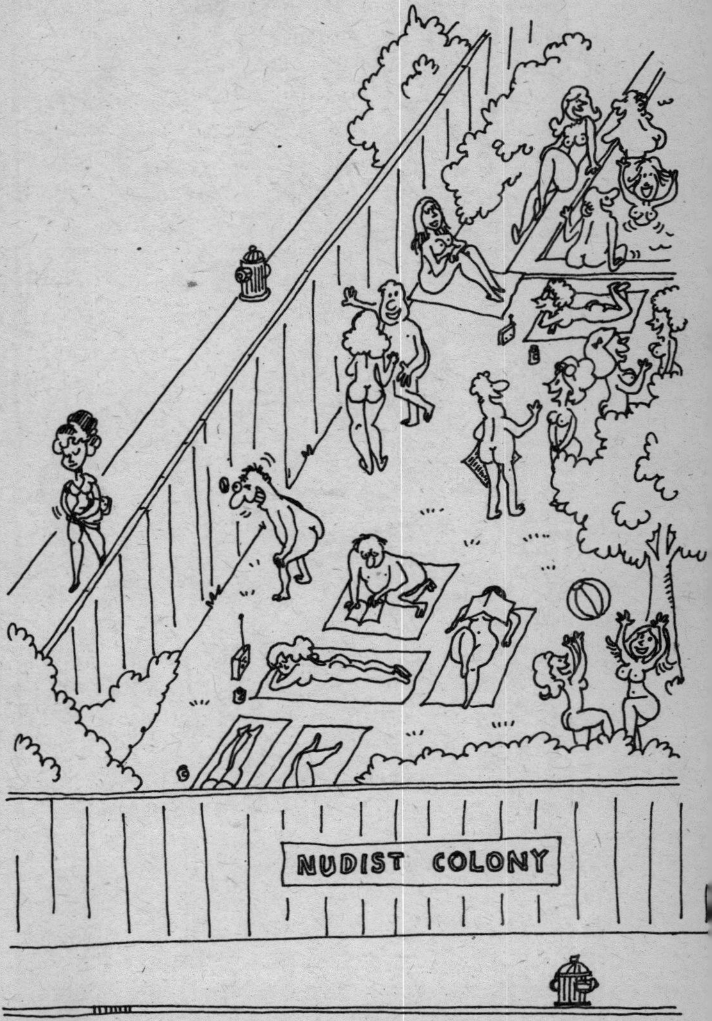
NUDIST COLONY

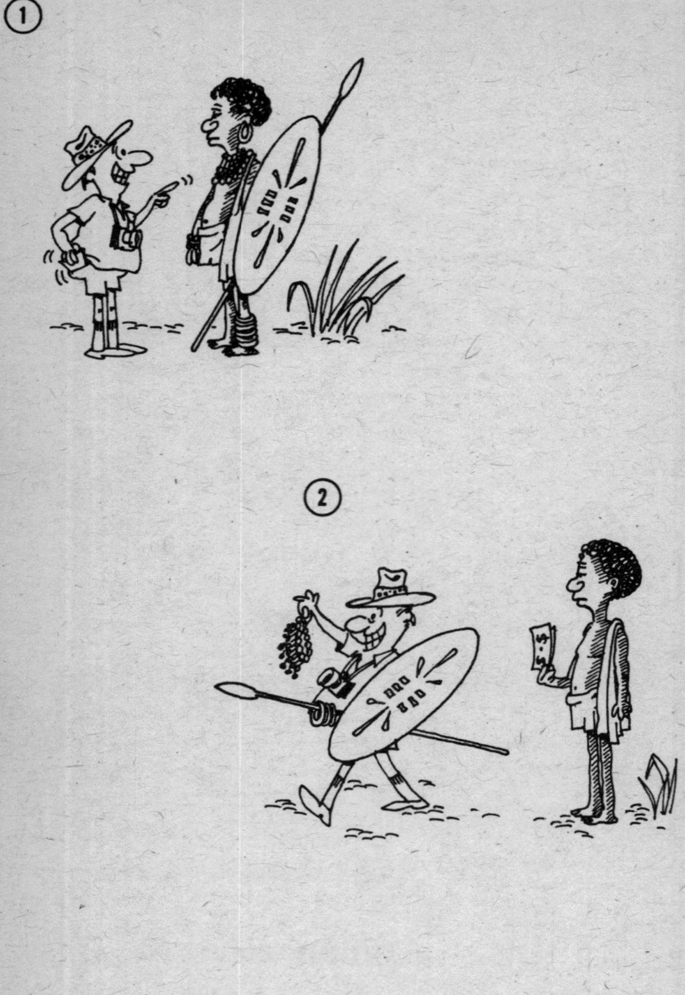

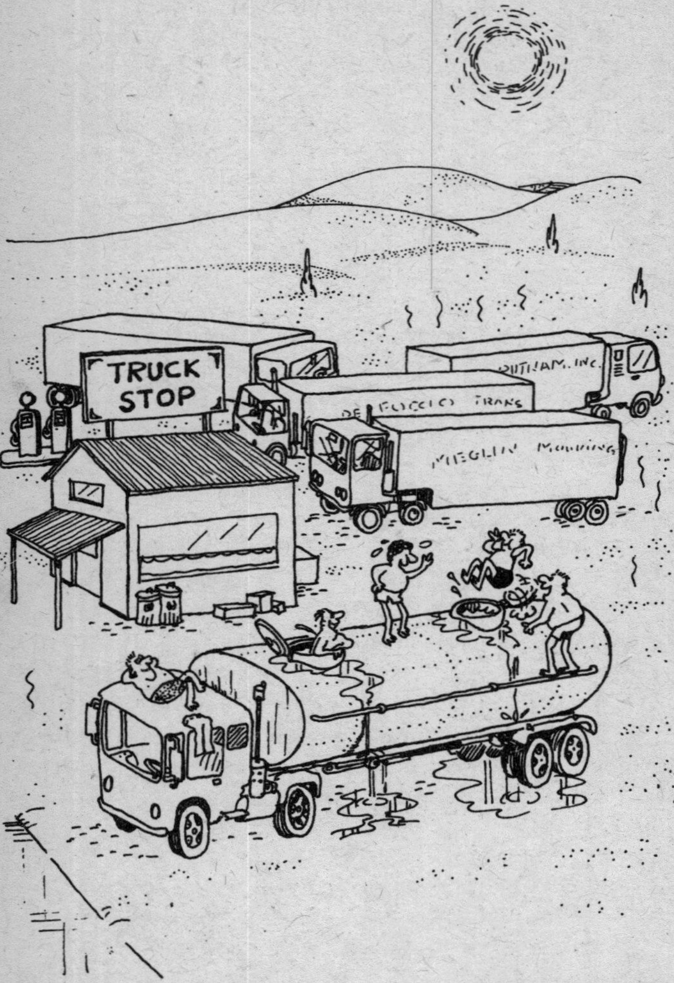
TRUCK
STOP

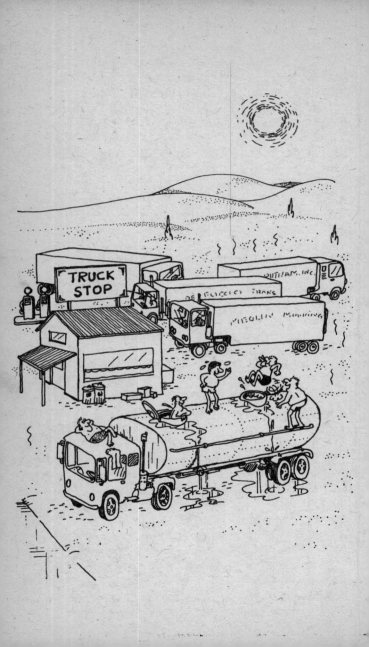

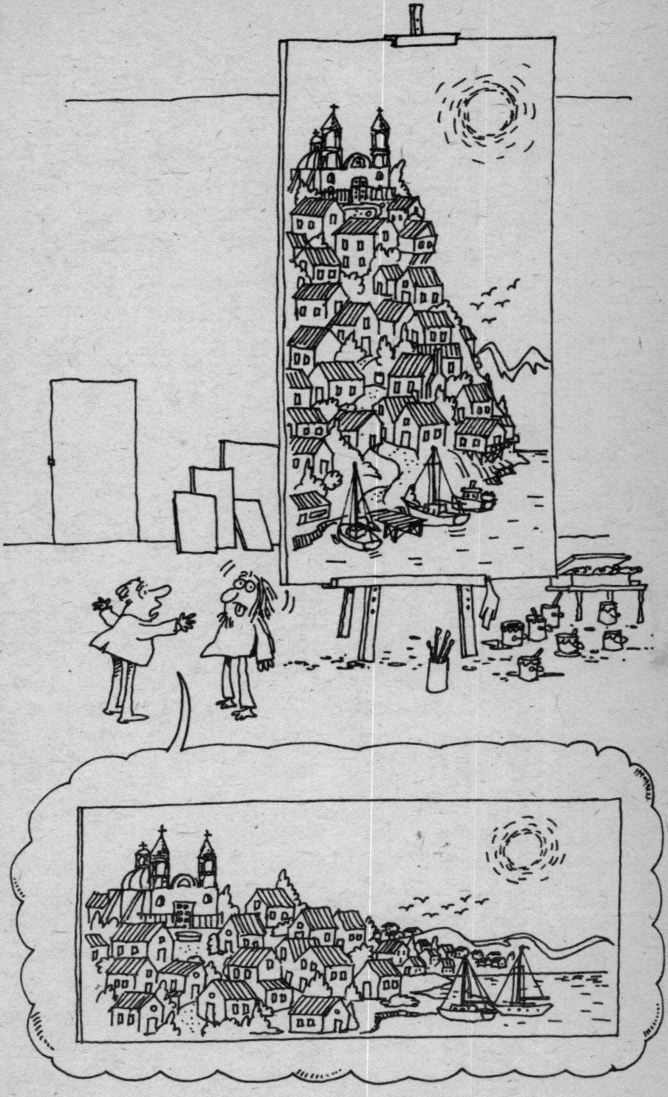

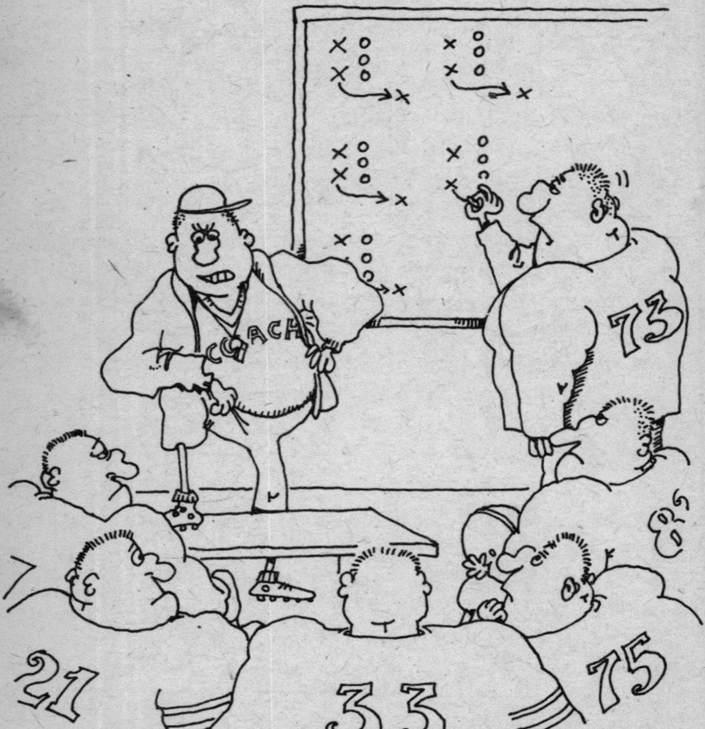
COACH
73
21
33
75

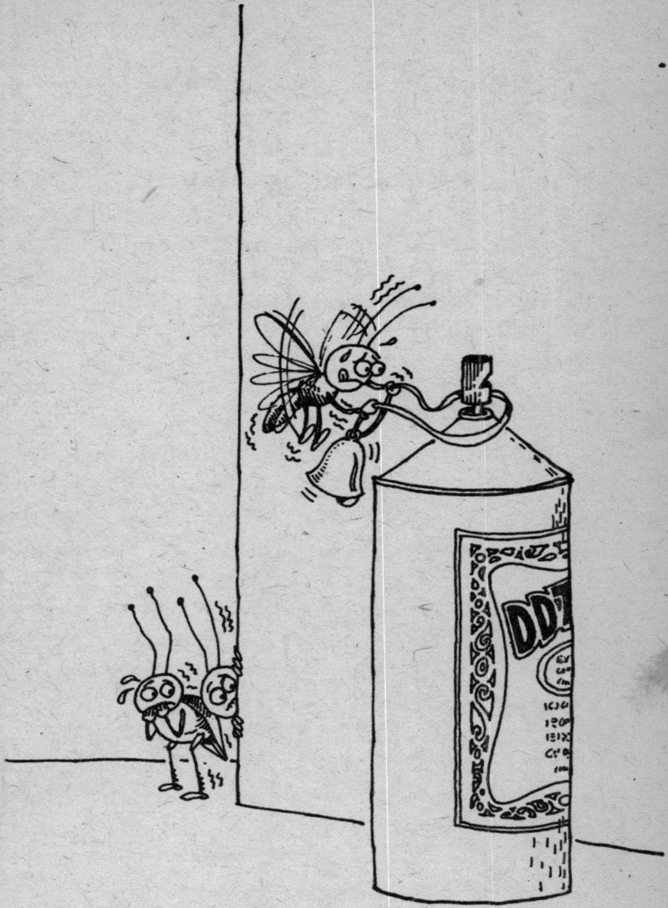

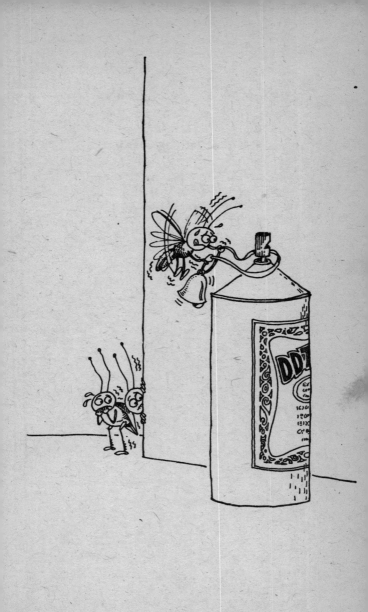

1

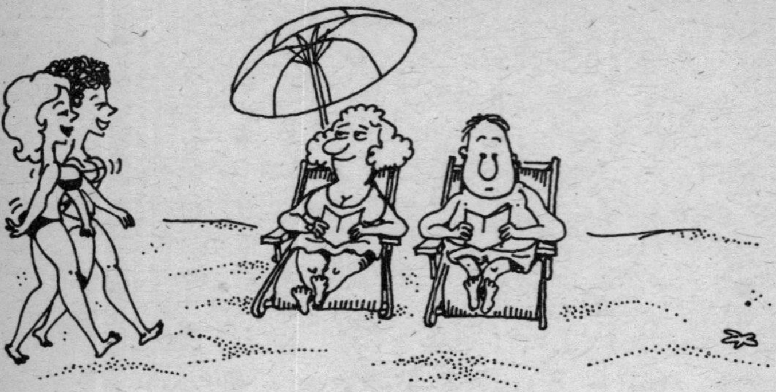

2

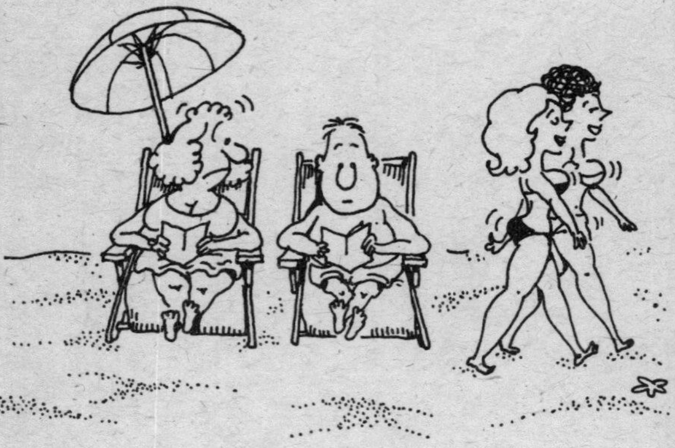

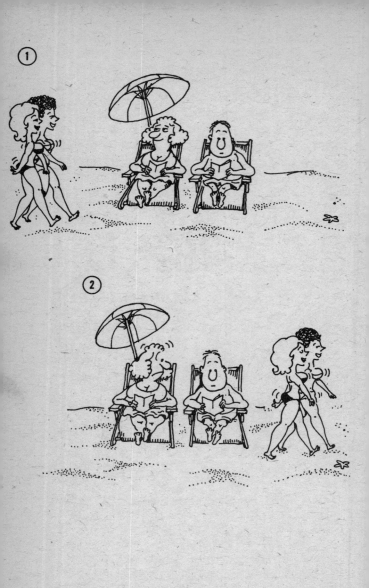

1

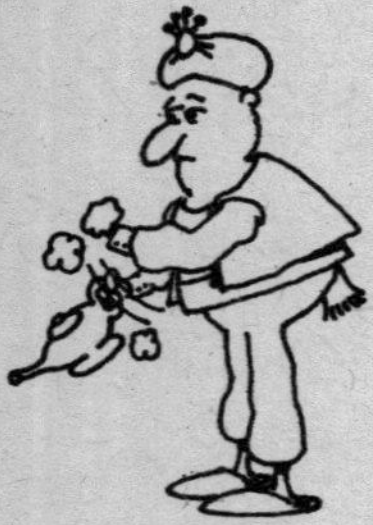

2

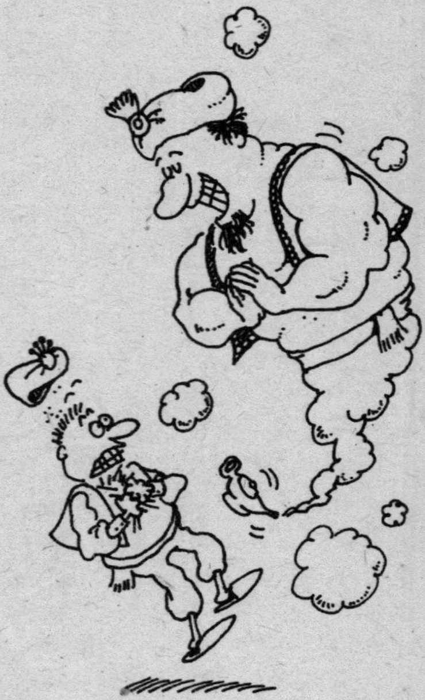

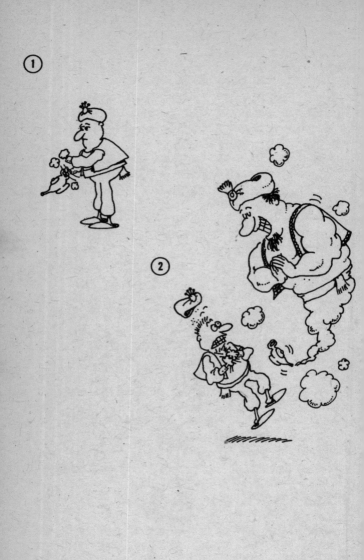

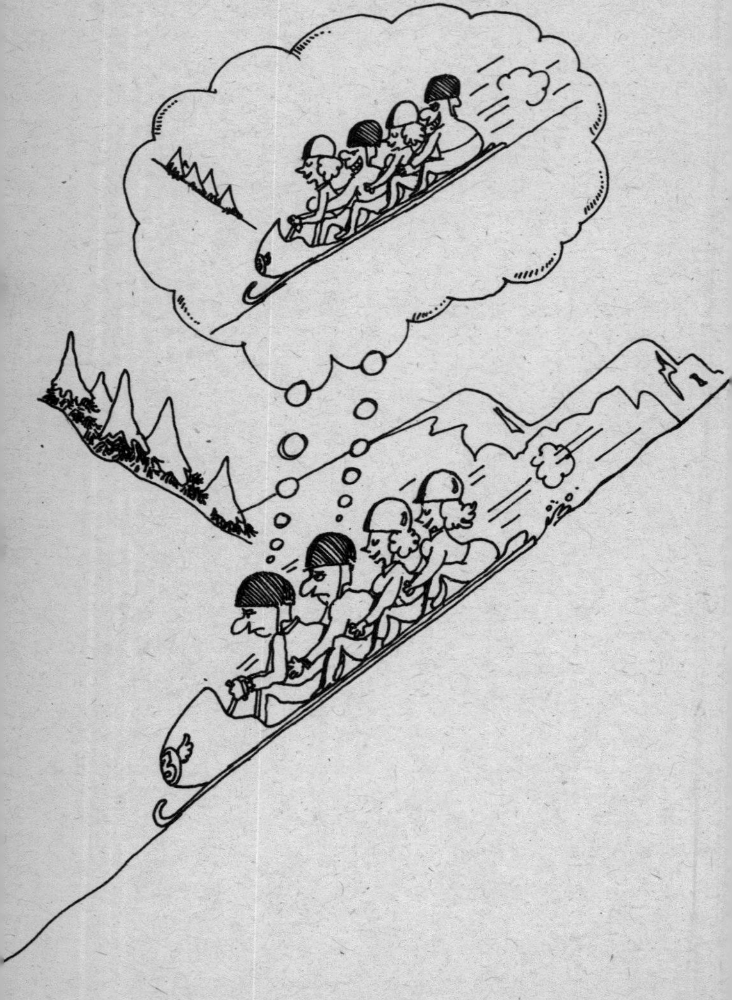

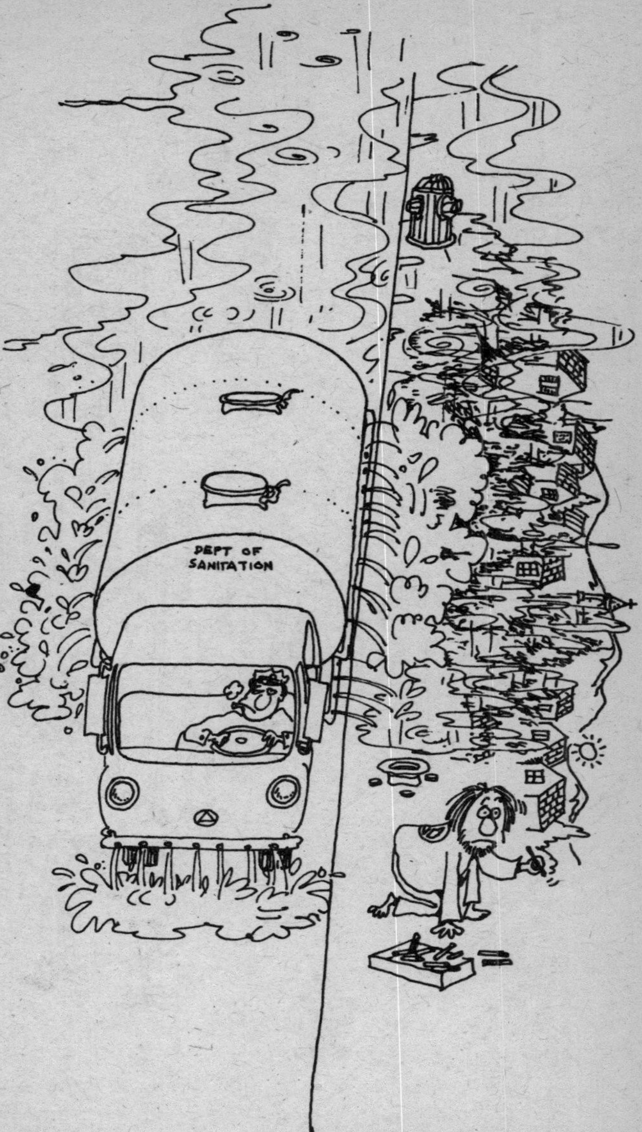
DEPT OF
SANITATION

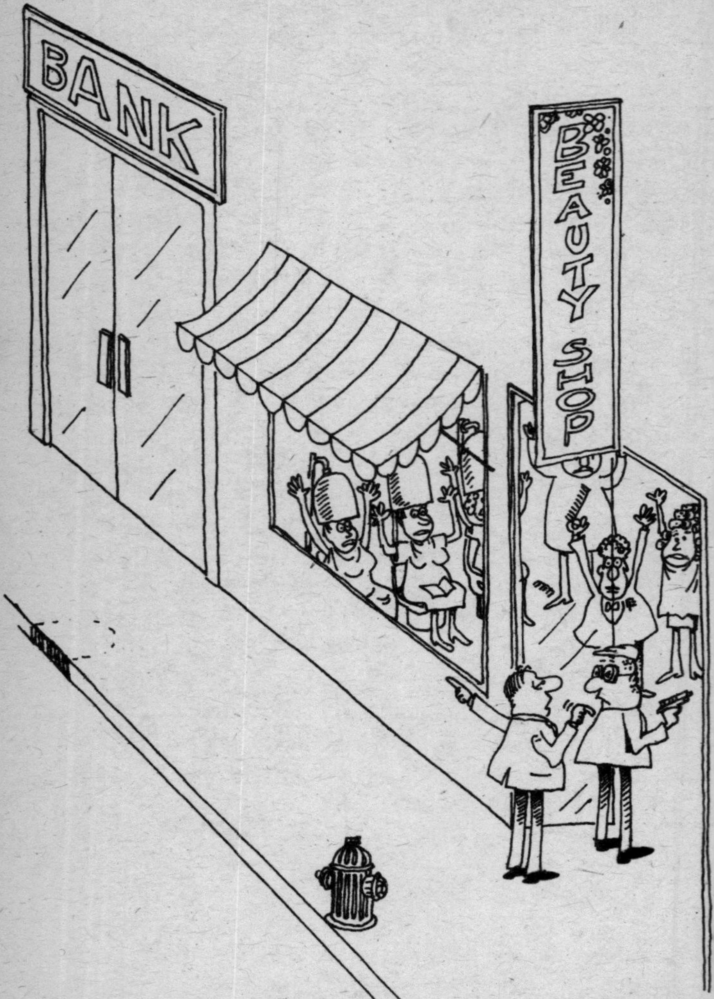
BANK
BEAUTY SHOP

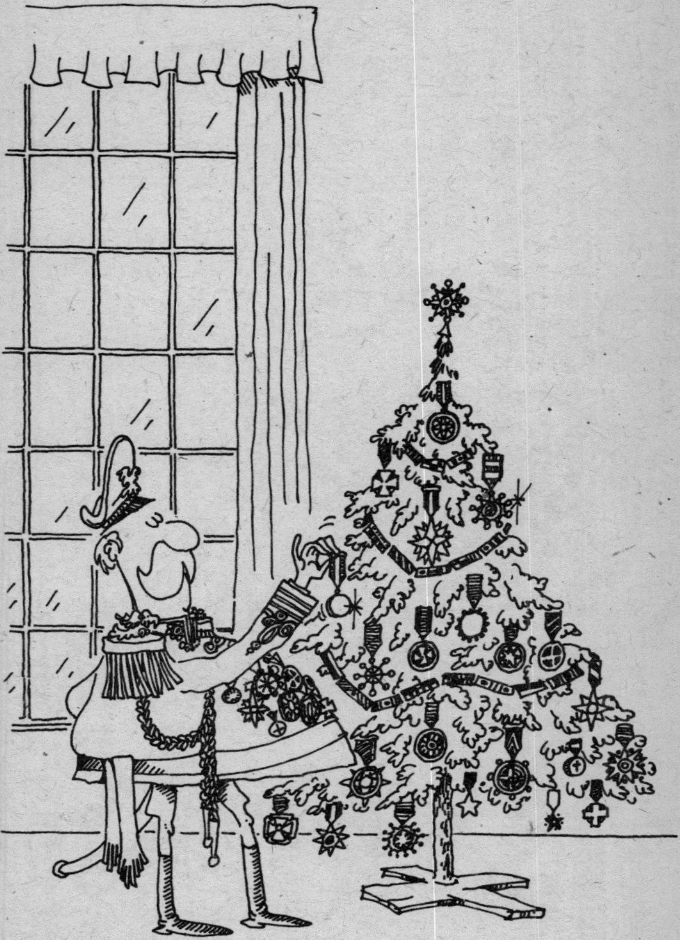

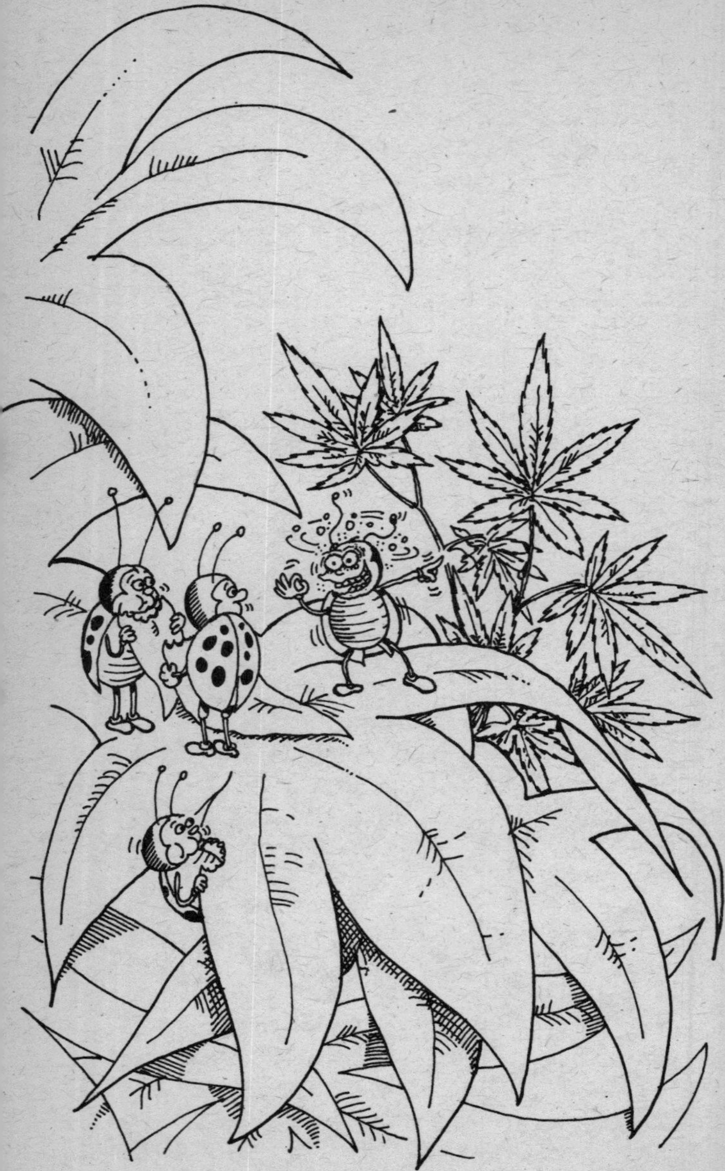

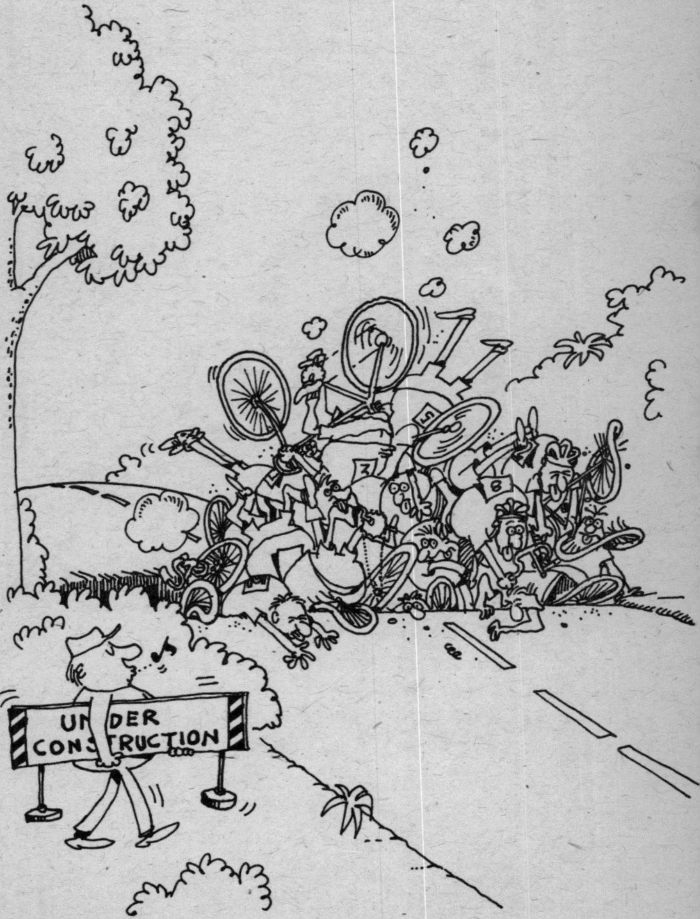
UN DER
CONS TRUCTION

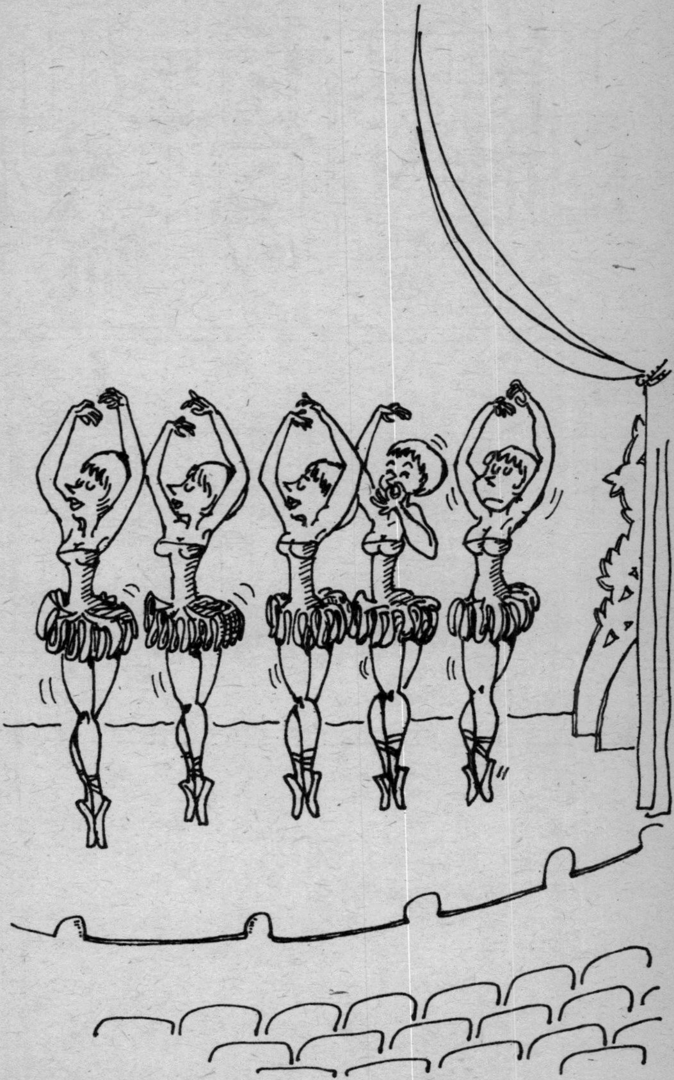

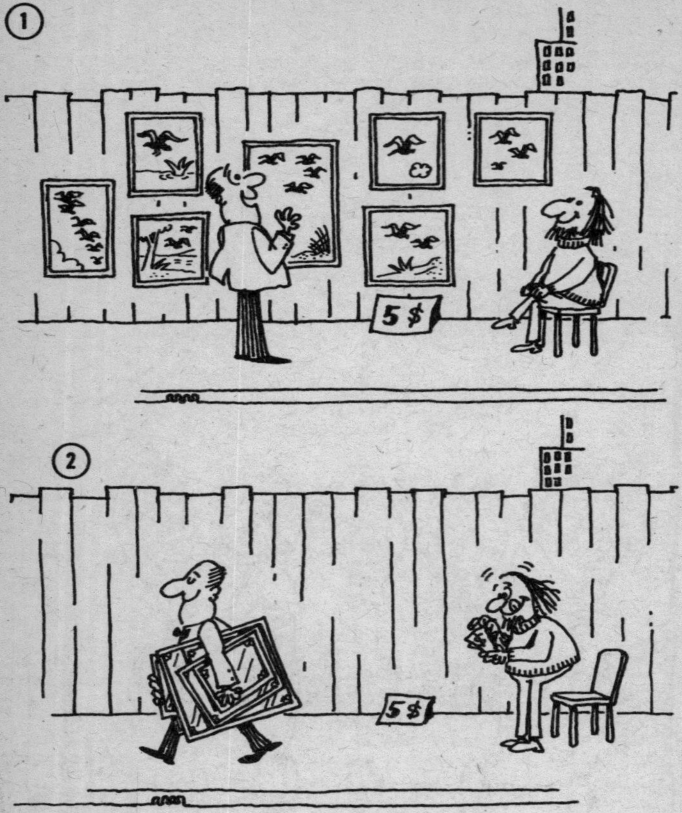
1
5 $
2
5 $

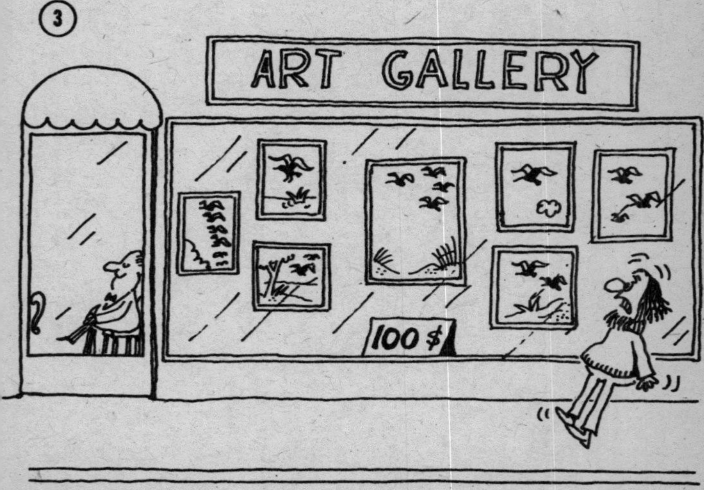
3
ART GALLERY
100 $

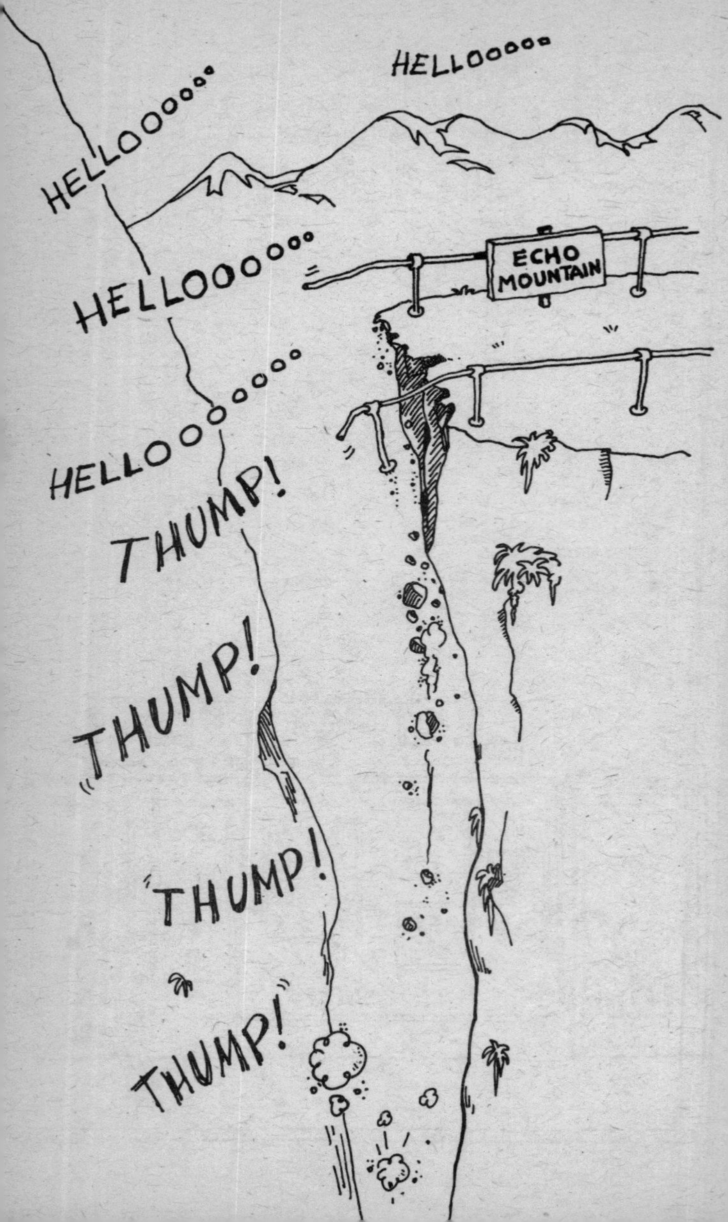
HELLOOOOO
HELLOOOOOO
HELLOOOOOOO
HELLOOOOOOO
ECHO MOUNTAIN
THUMP!
THUMP!
THUMP!
THUMP!

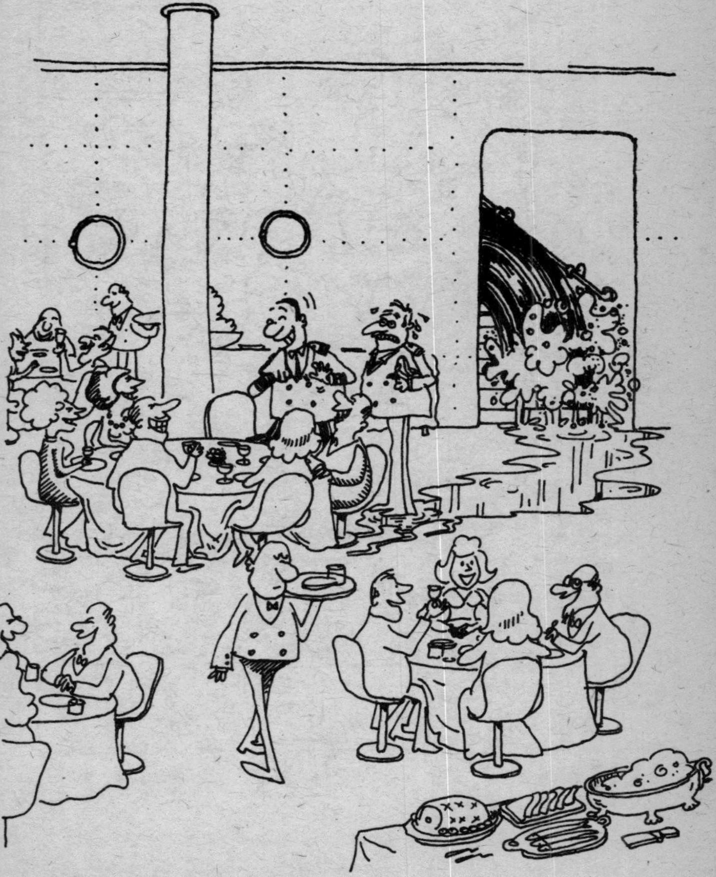

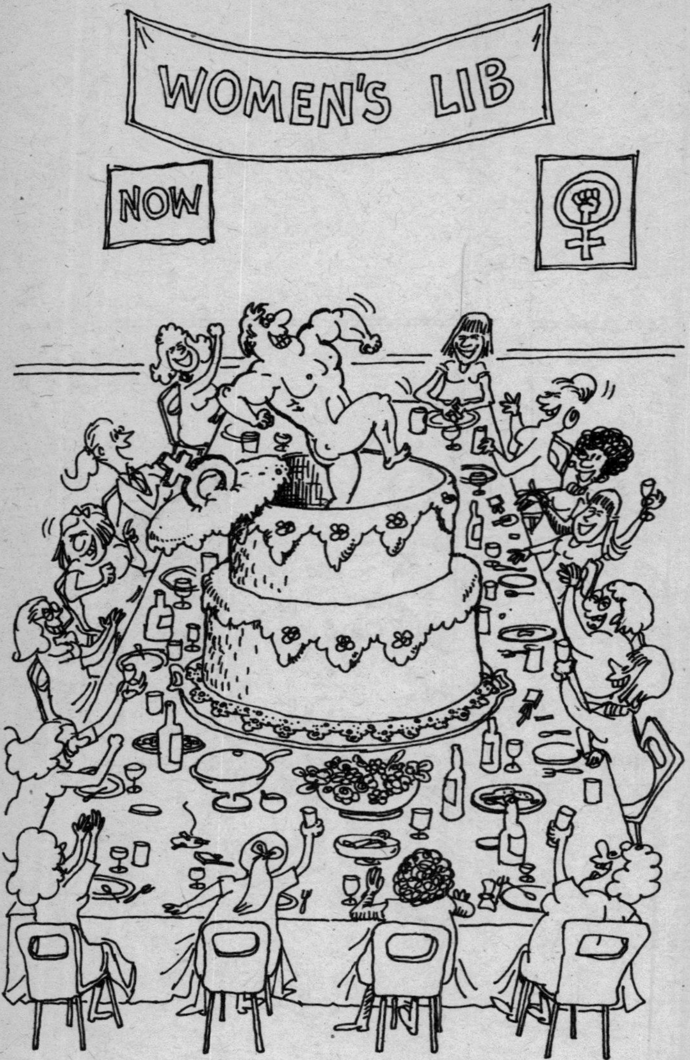
WOMEN'S LIB
NOW

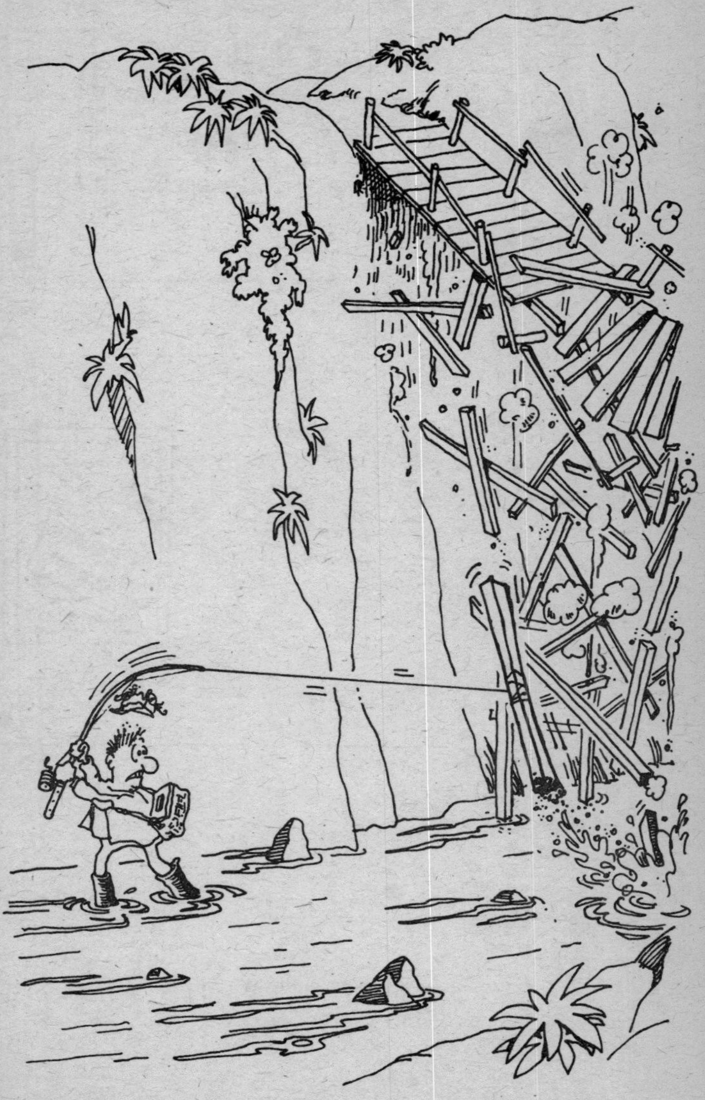

1

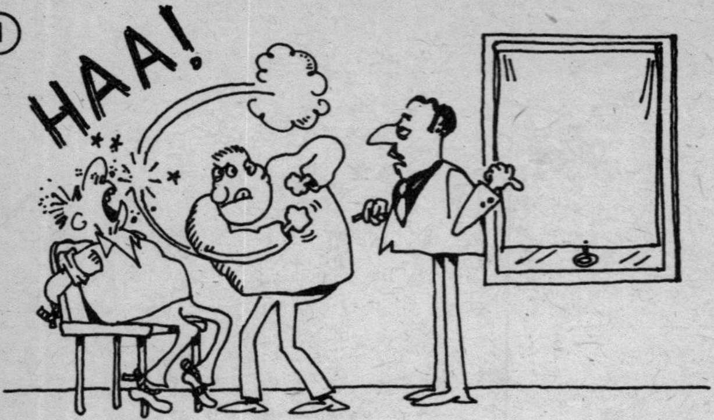
HAA!

2

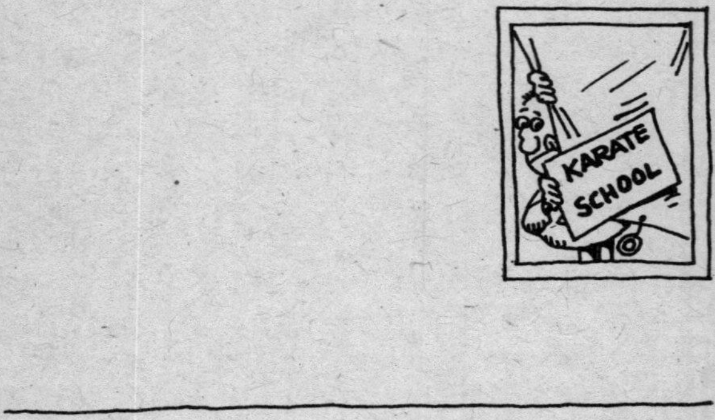
KARATE
SCHOOL

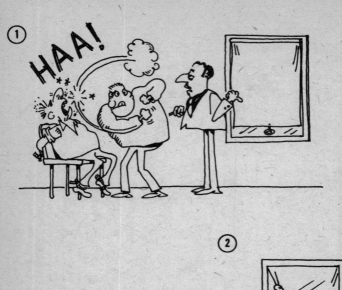

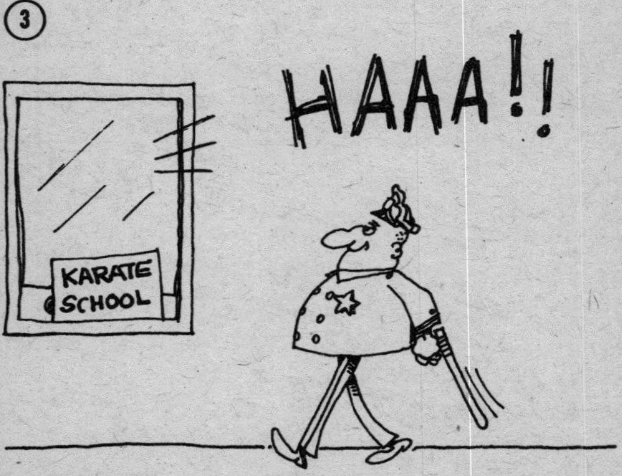
3
HAAA!!
KARATE SCHOOL

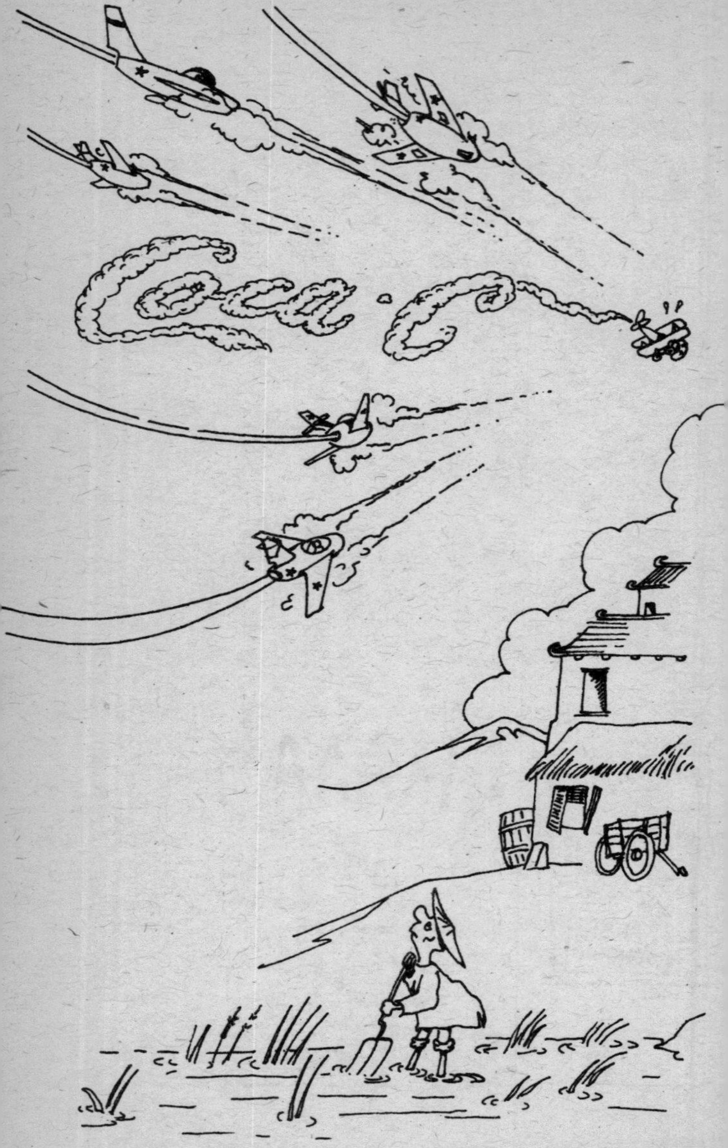
Coca-C

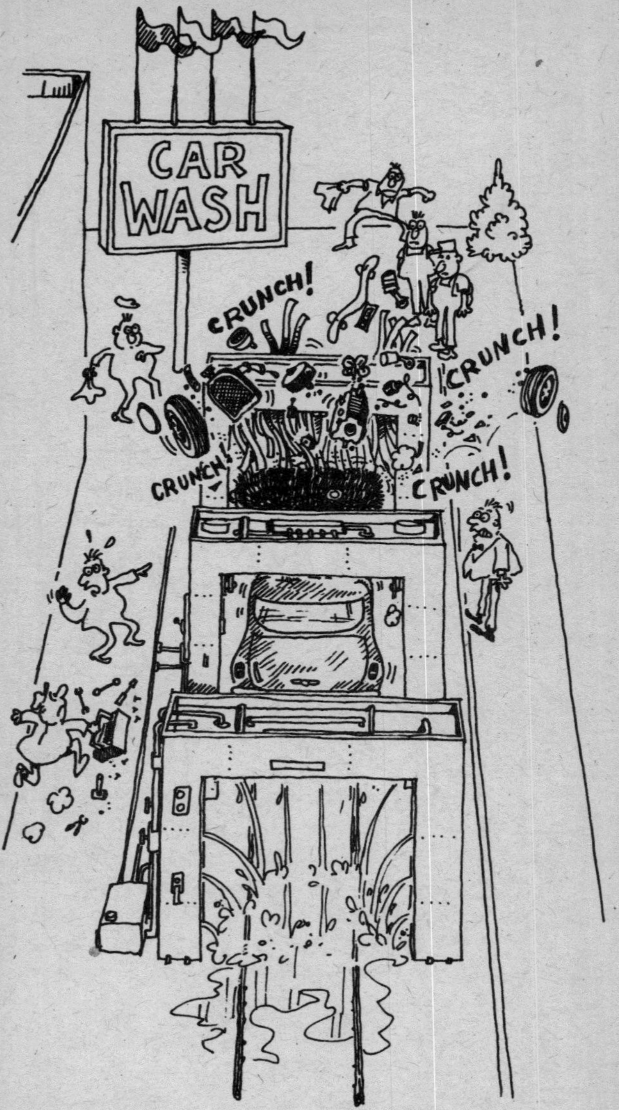
CAR WASH
CRUNCH!
CRUNCH!
CRUNCH!
CRUNCH!

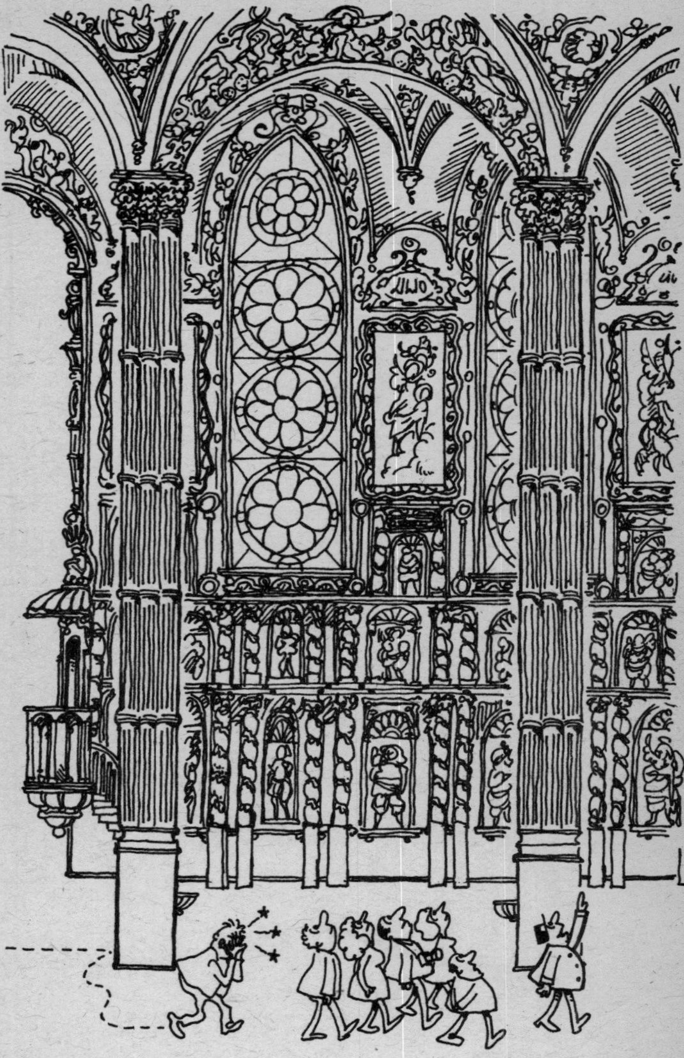

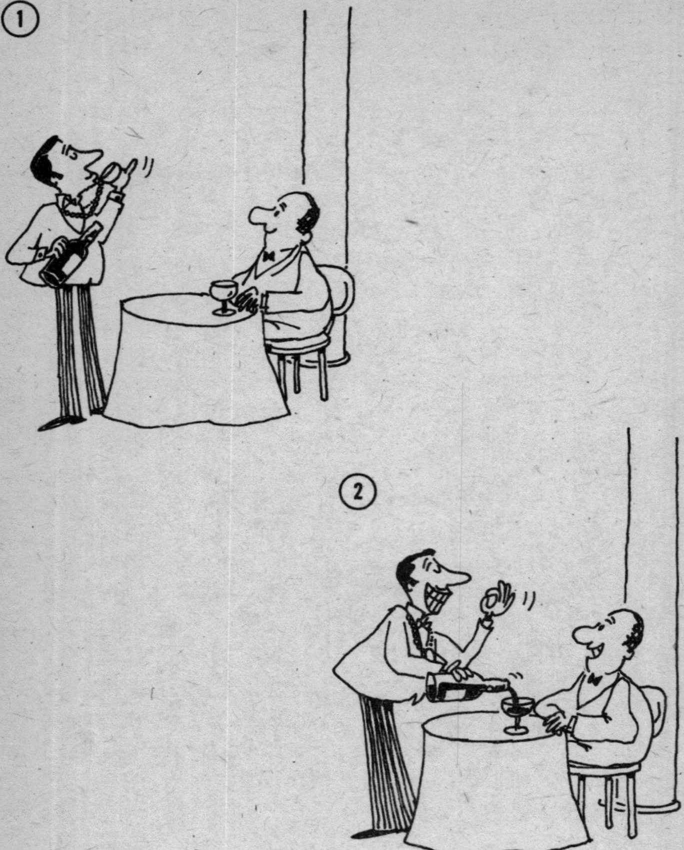
1
2

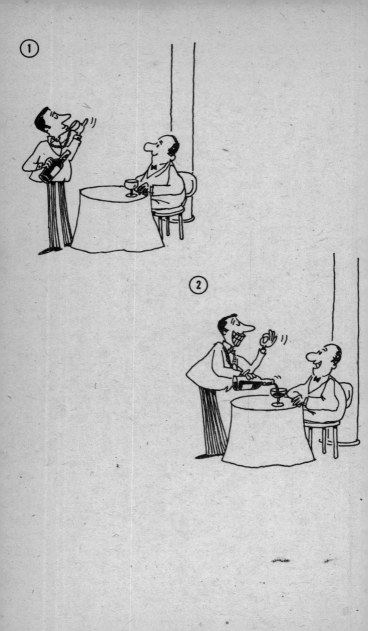

③

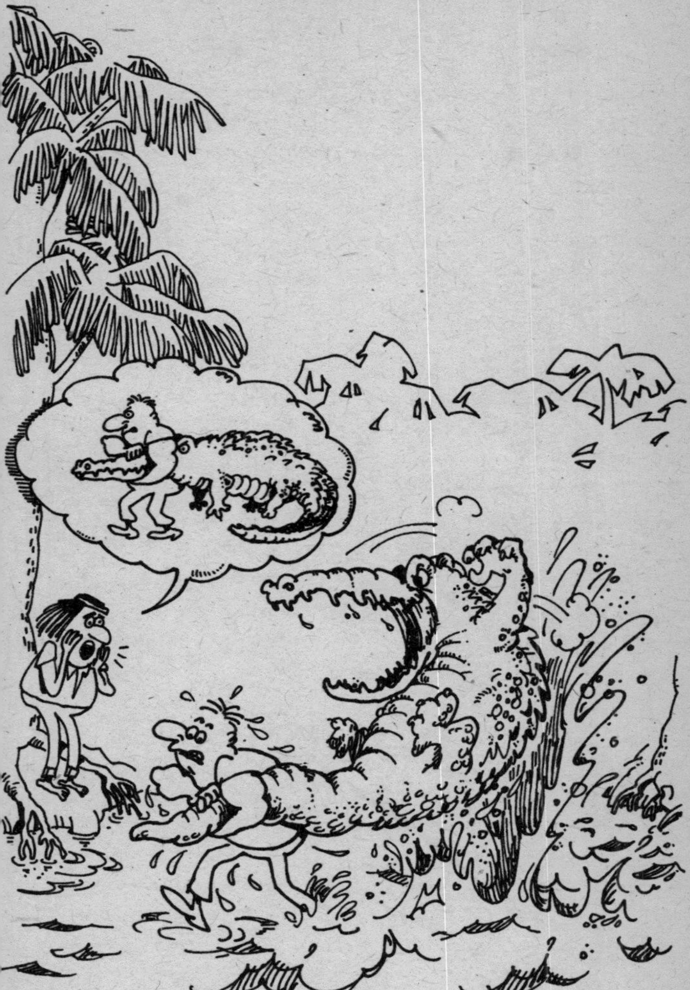

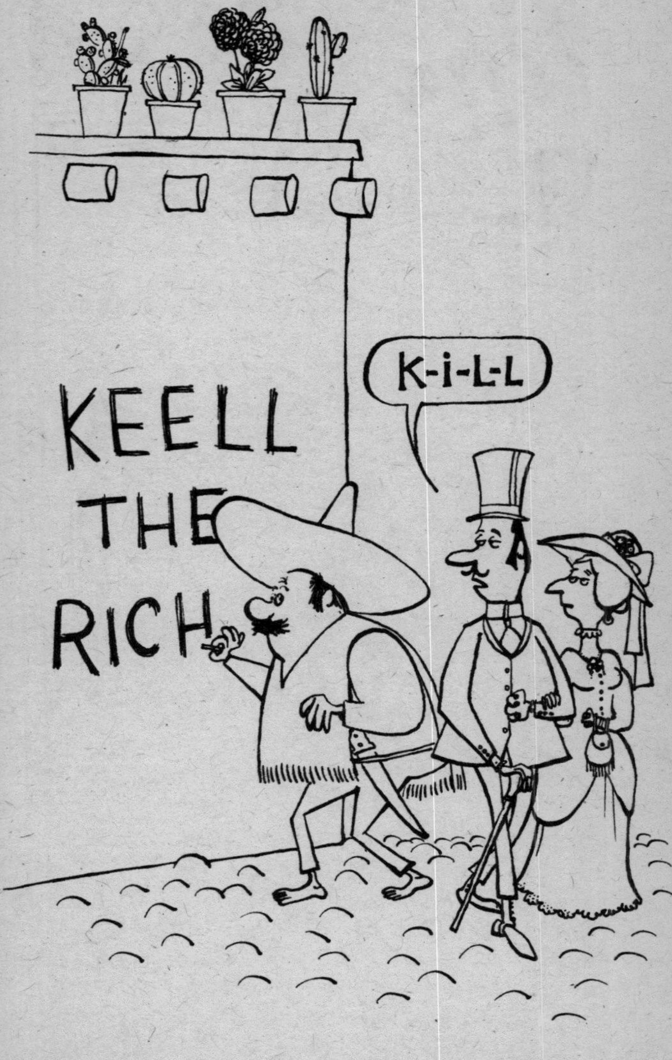
K-i-L-L
KEELL
THE
RICH

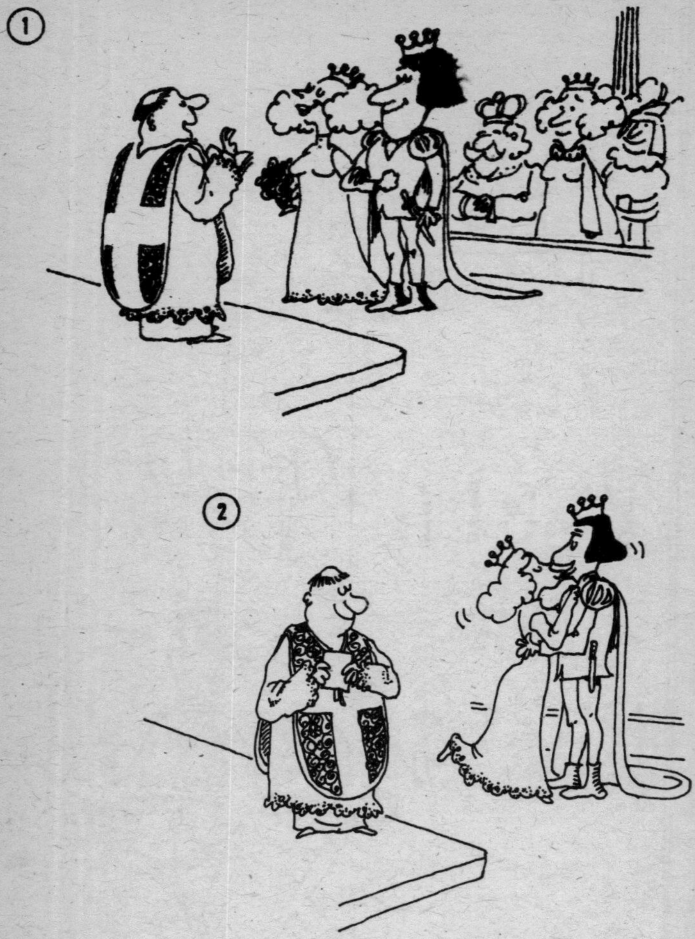
1
2

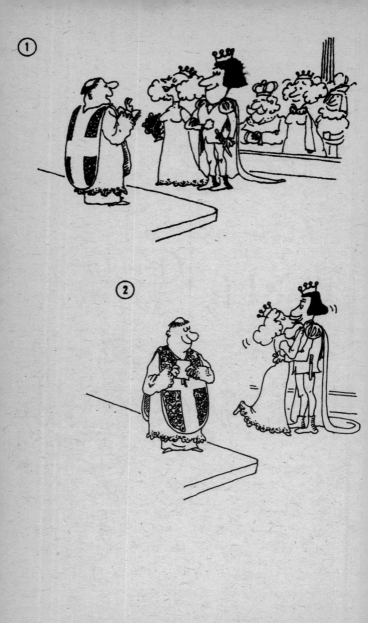

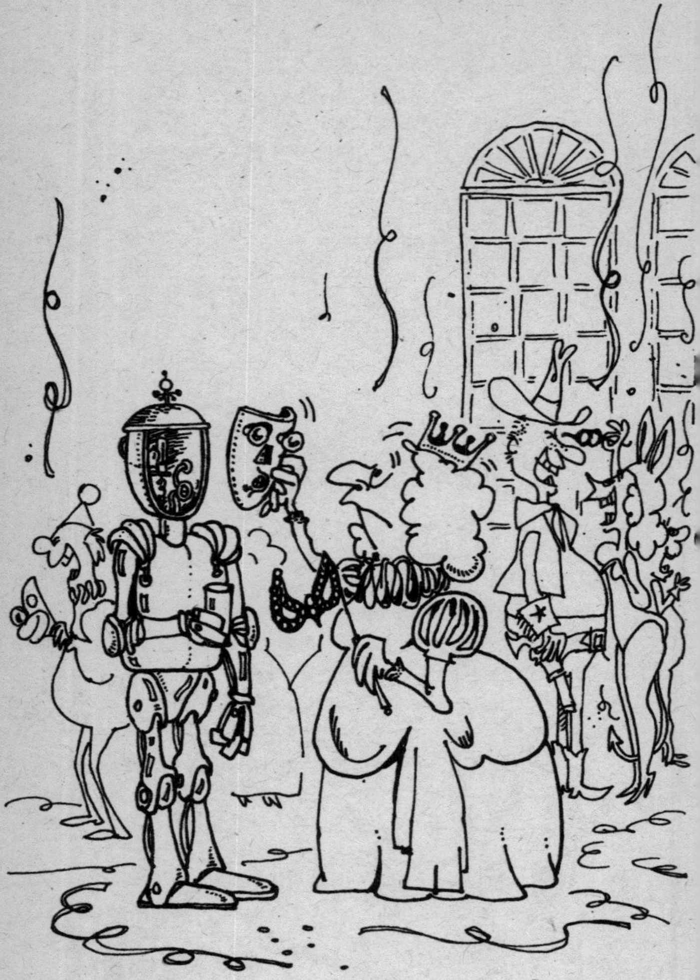

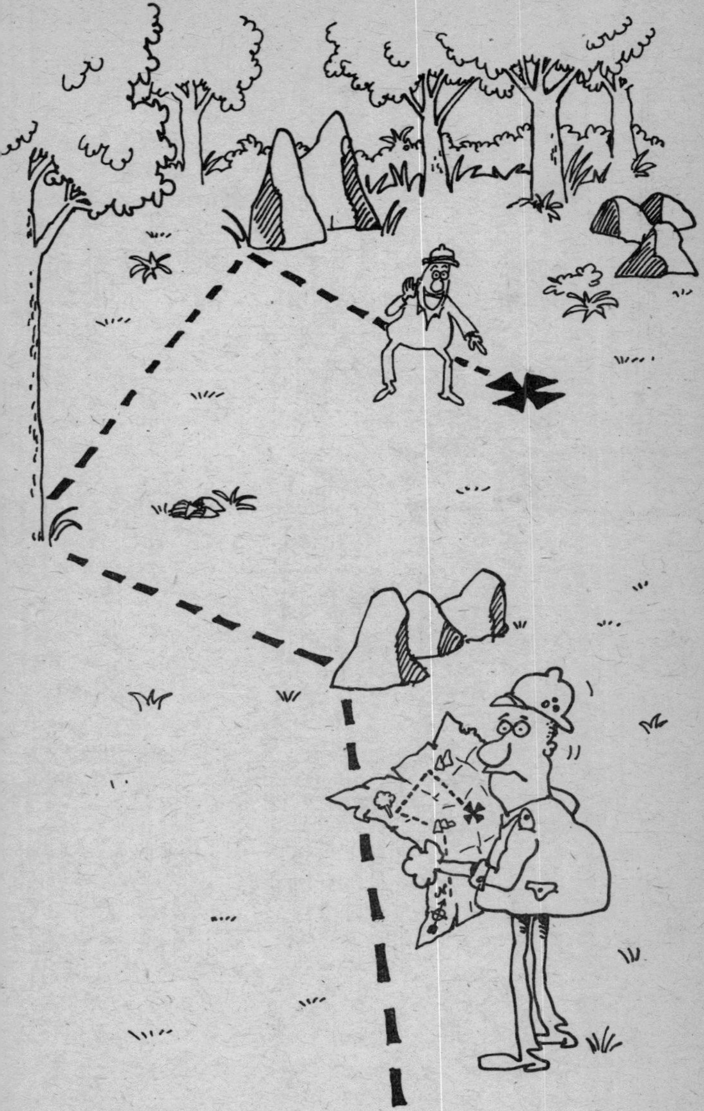

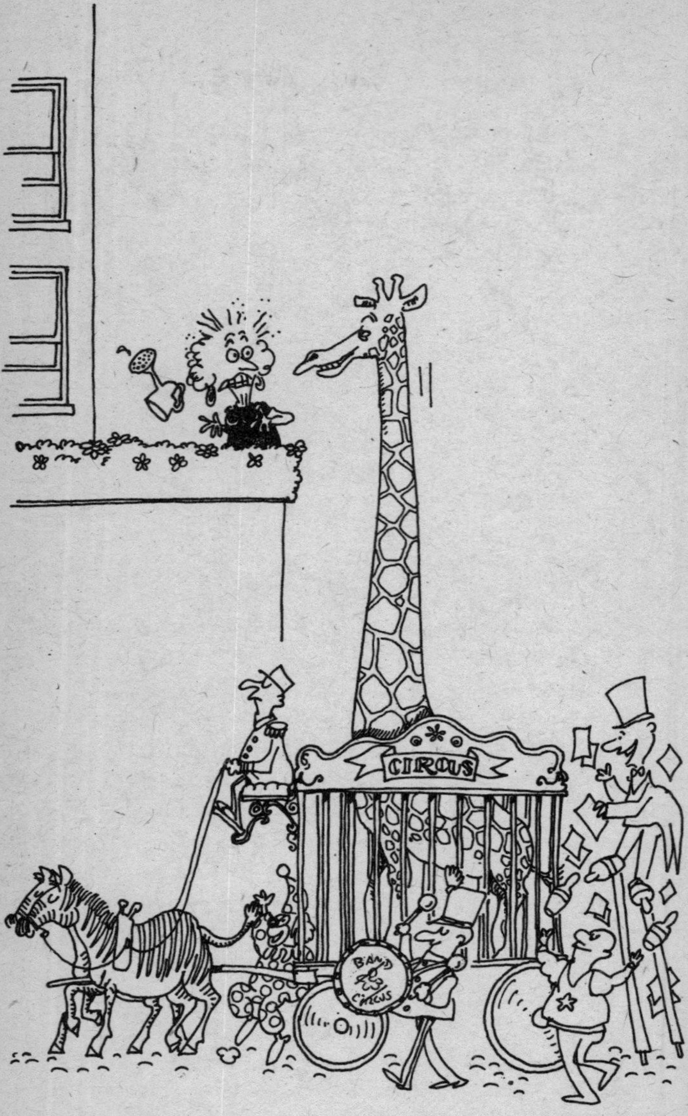
CIRCUS
BAND
CIRCUS

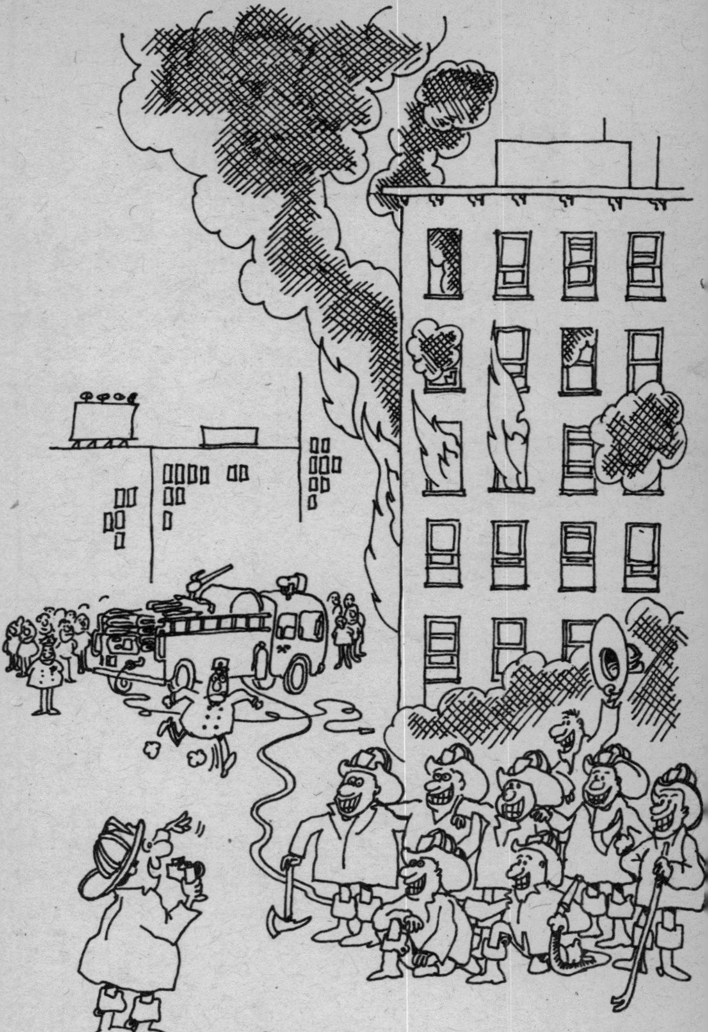

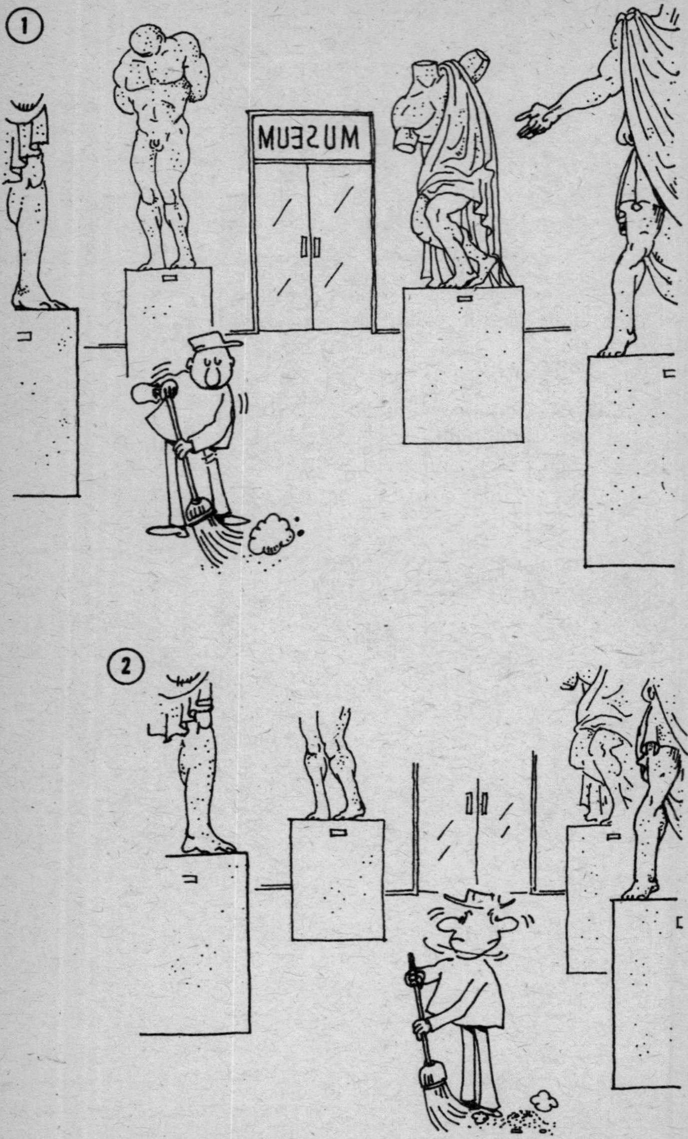
1
MUƎSUM
2

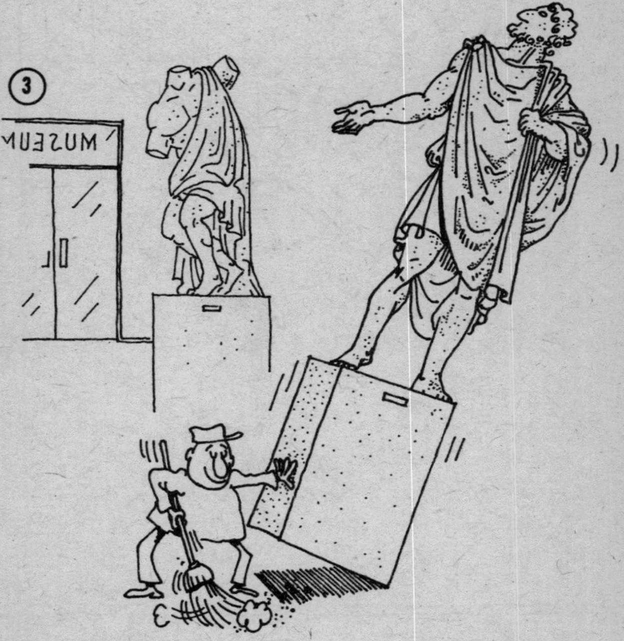
3
MUSEUM

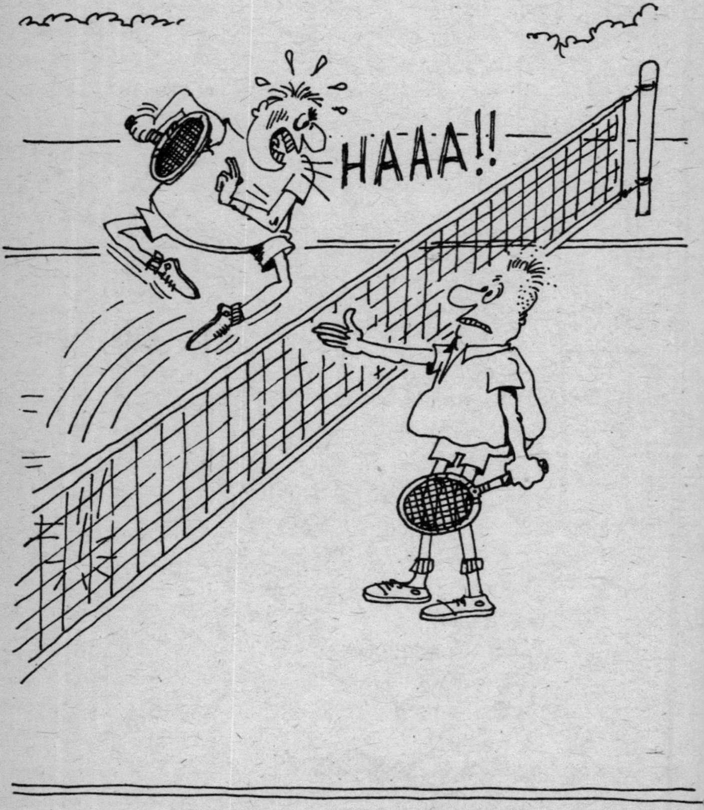
HAAA!!

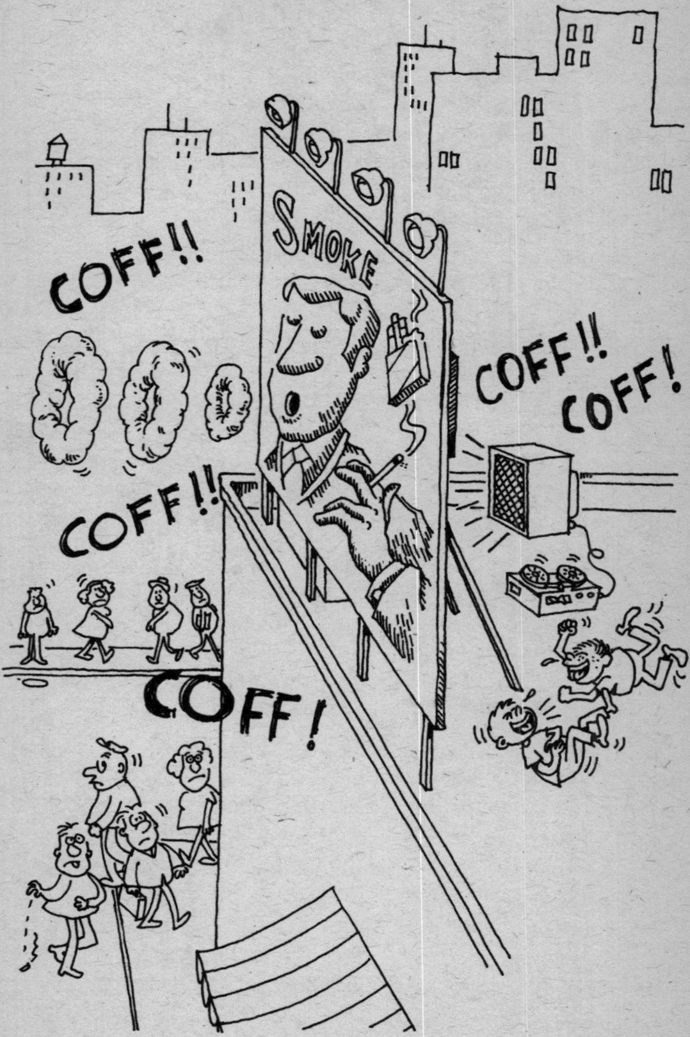
SMOKE
COFF!!
COFF!!
COFF!!
COFF!
COFF!

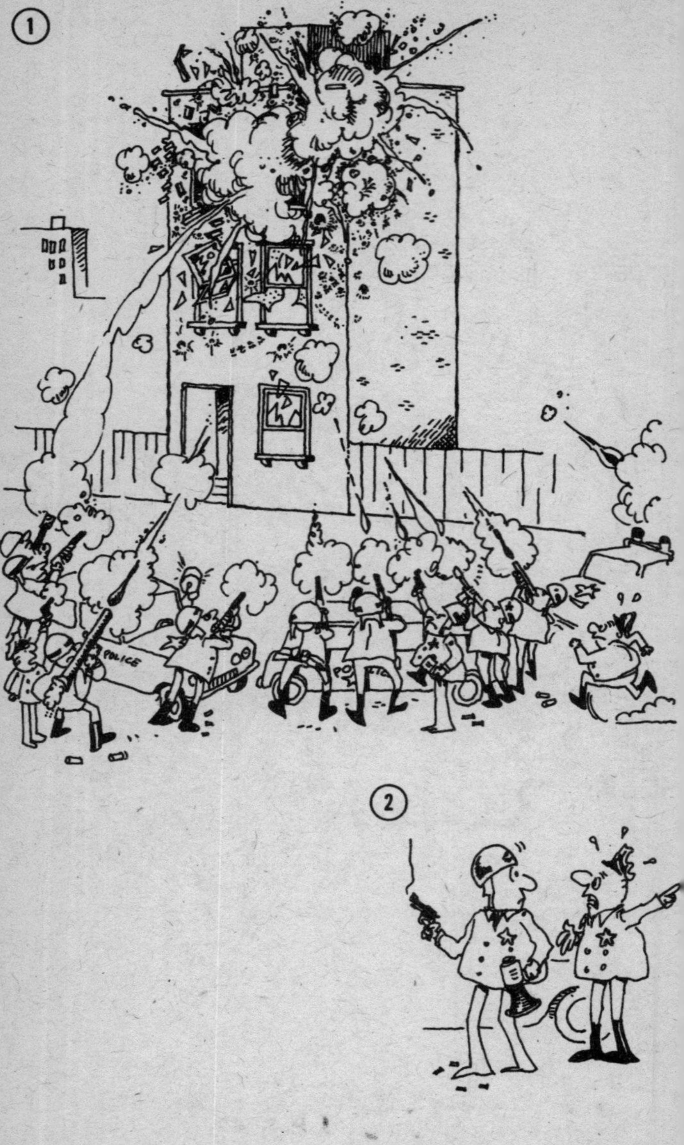
1
POLICE
2

3

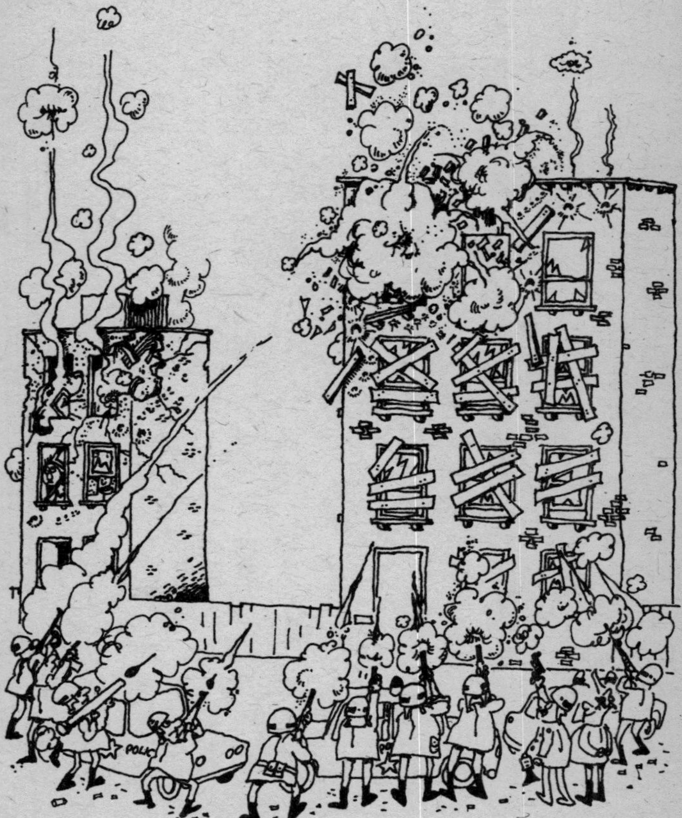

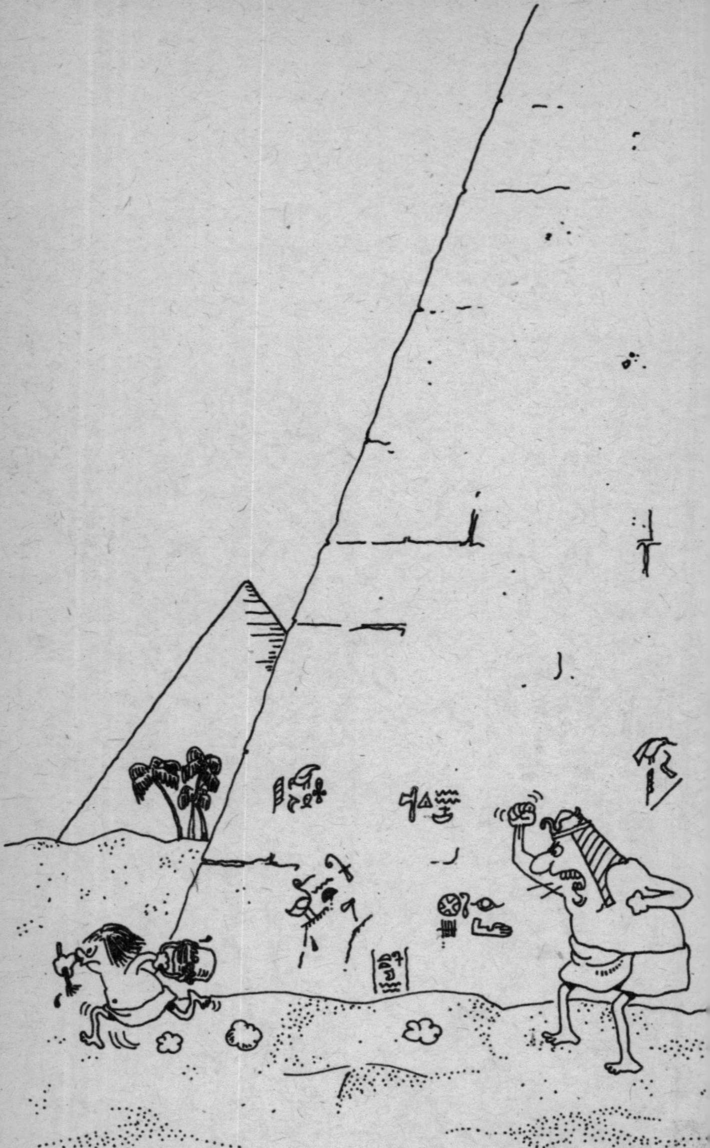

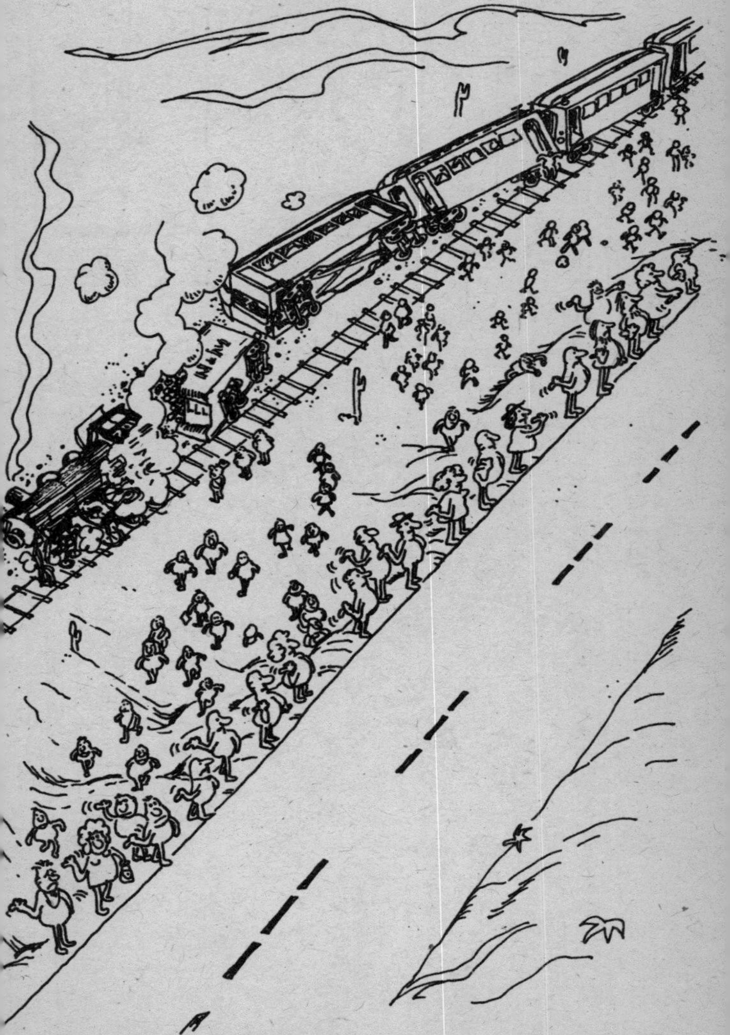

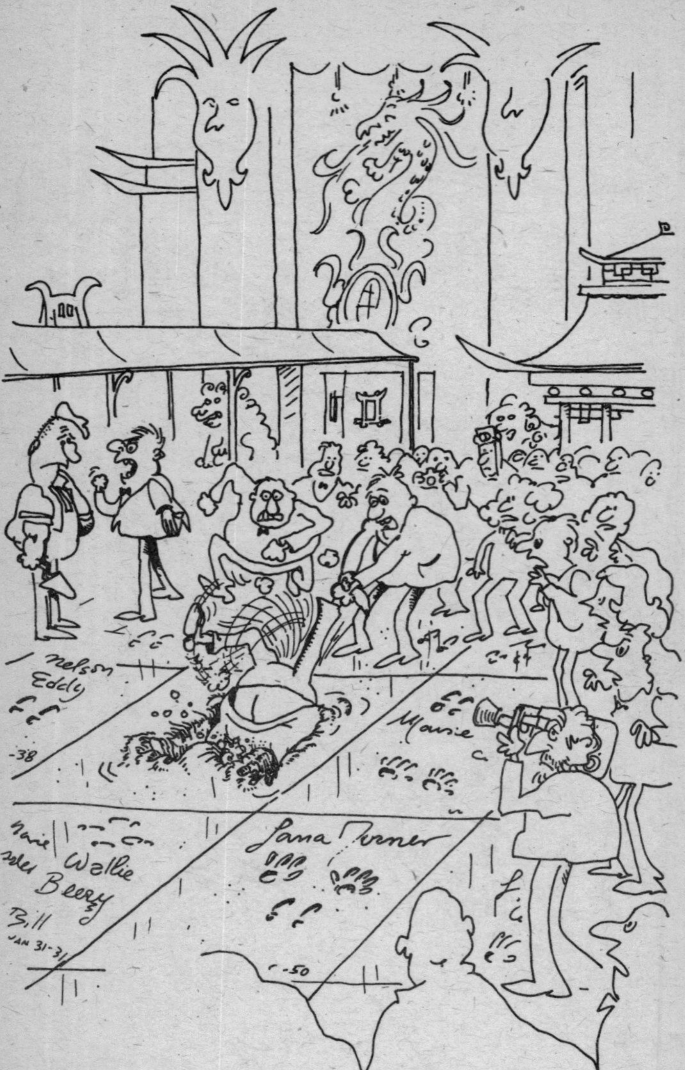
nelson Eddy
-38
Marie
Lana Turner
Wallie Beery
Bill
-50

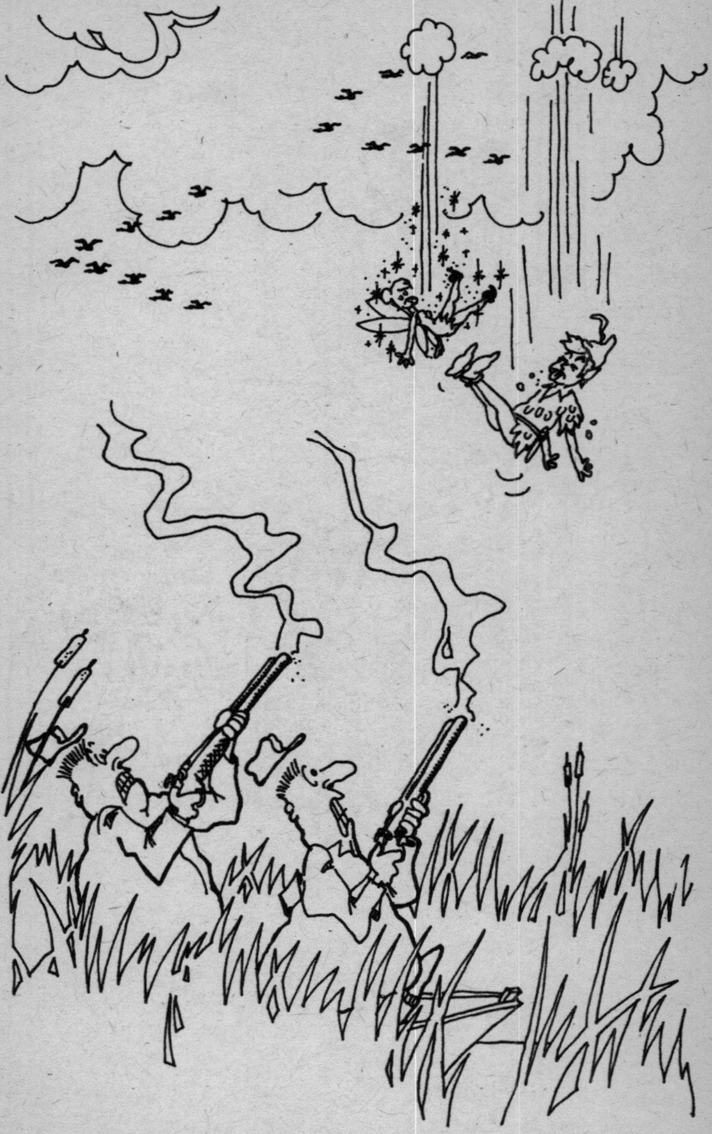

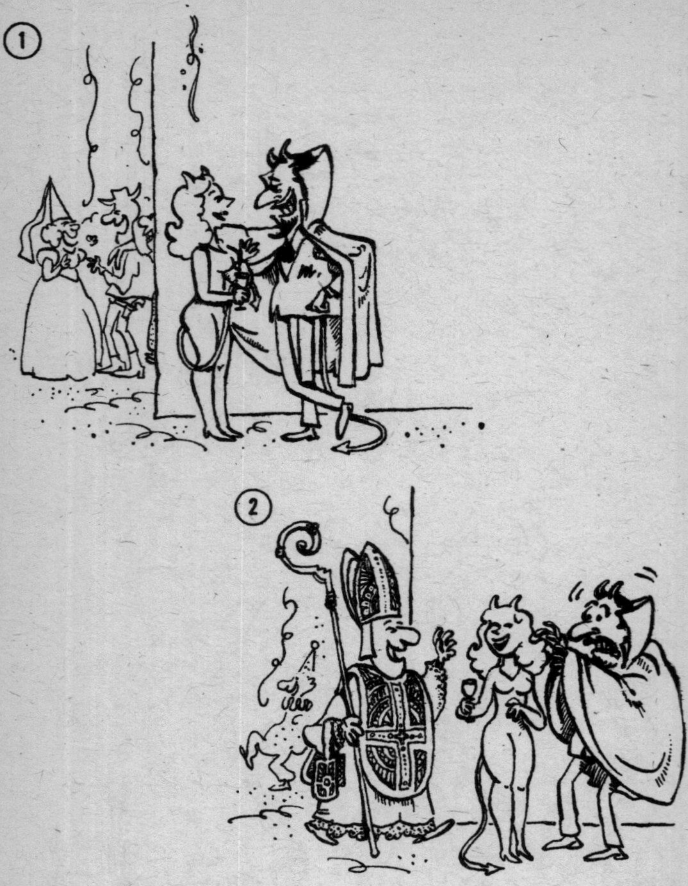

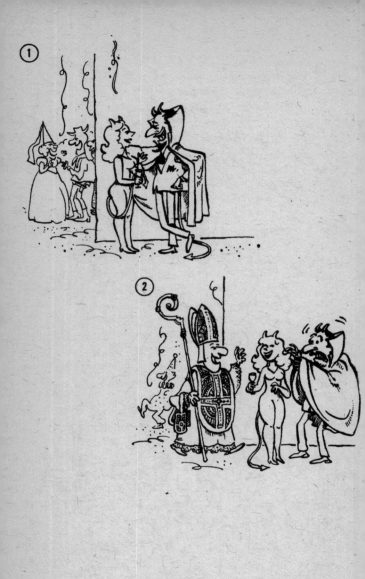

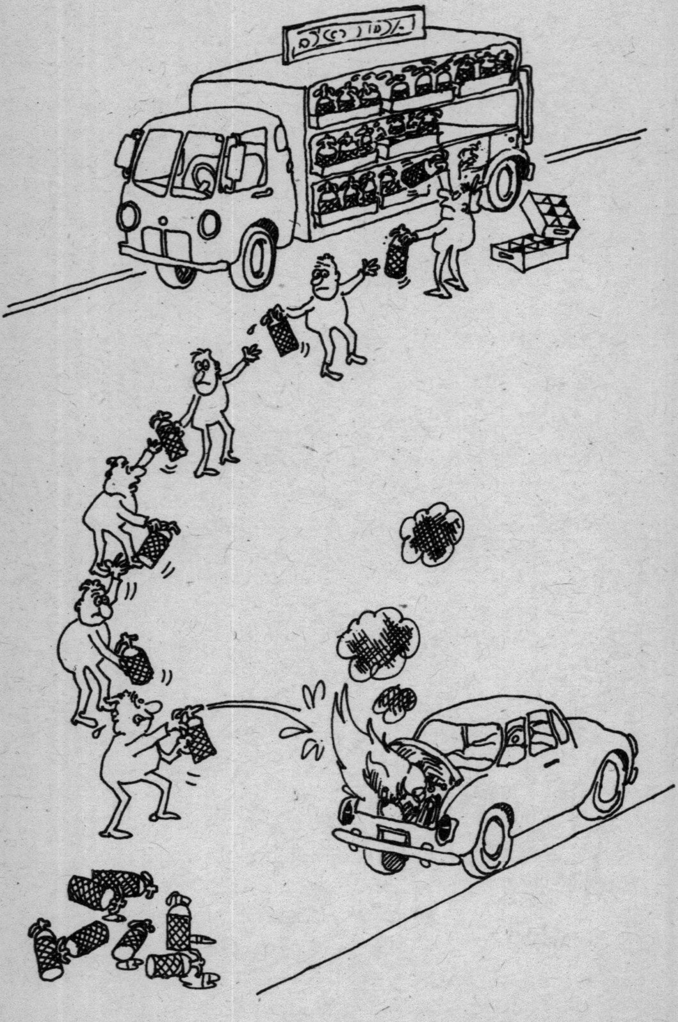

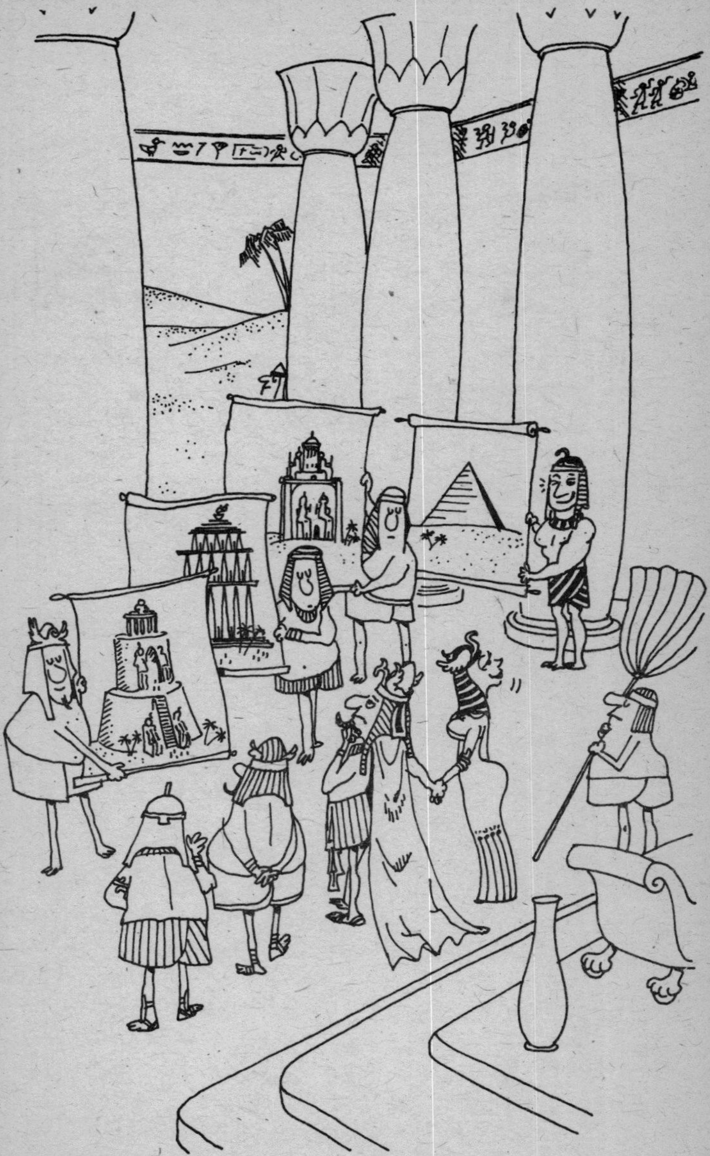

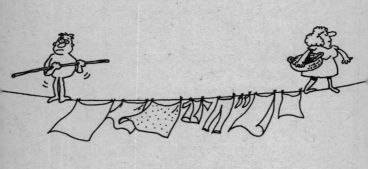

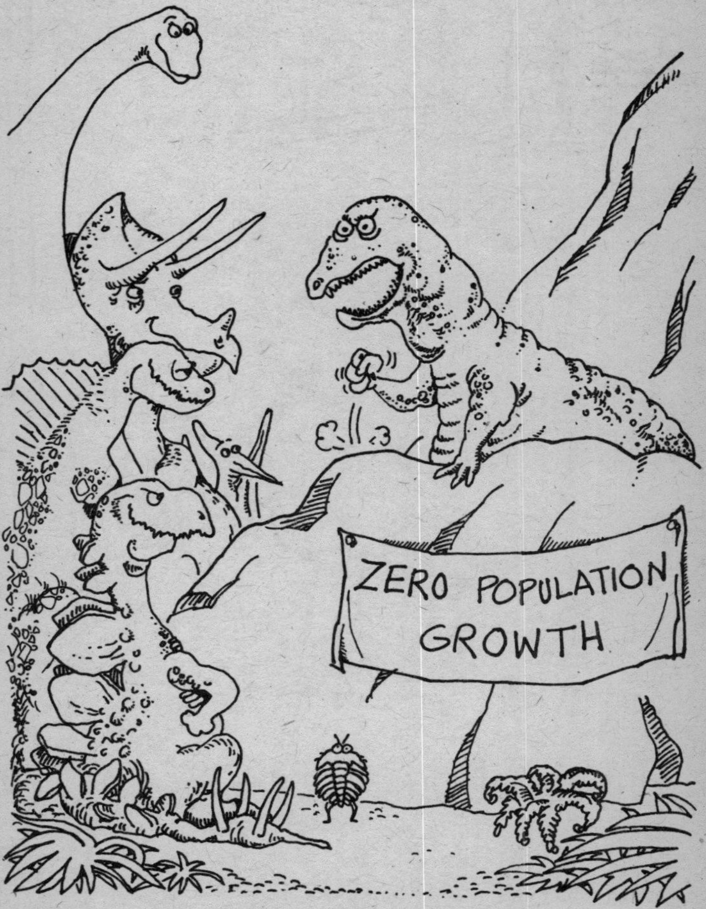
ZERO POPULATION
GROWTH

1

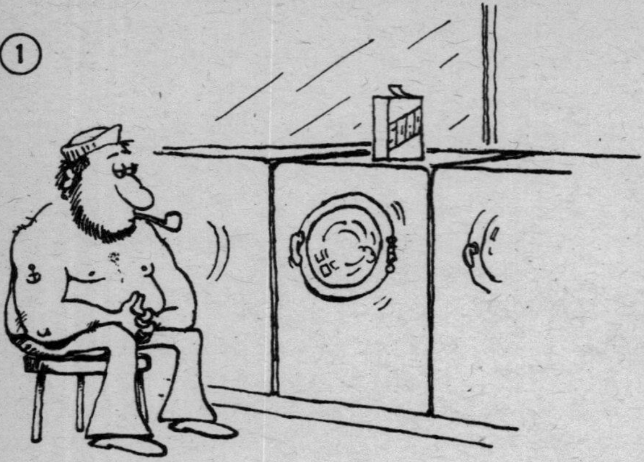

2

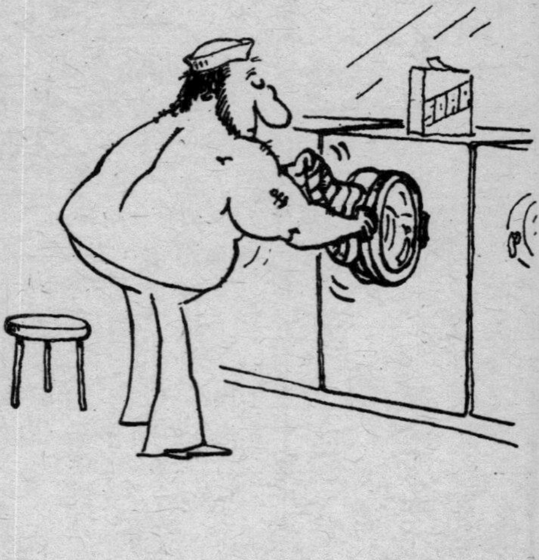
SOAP

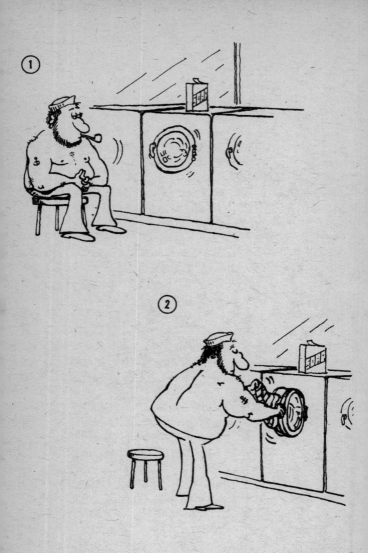

3

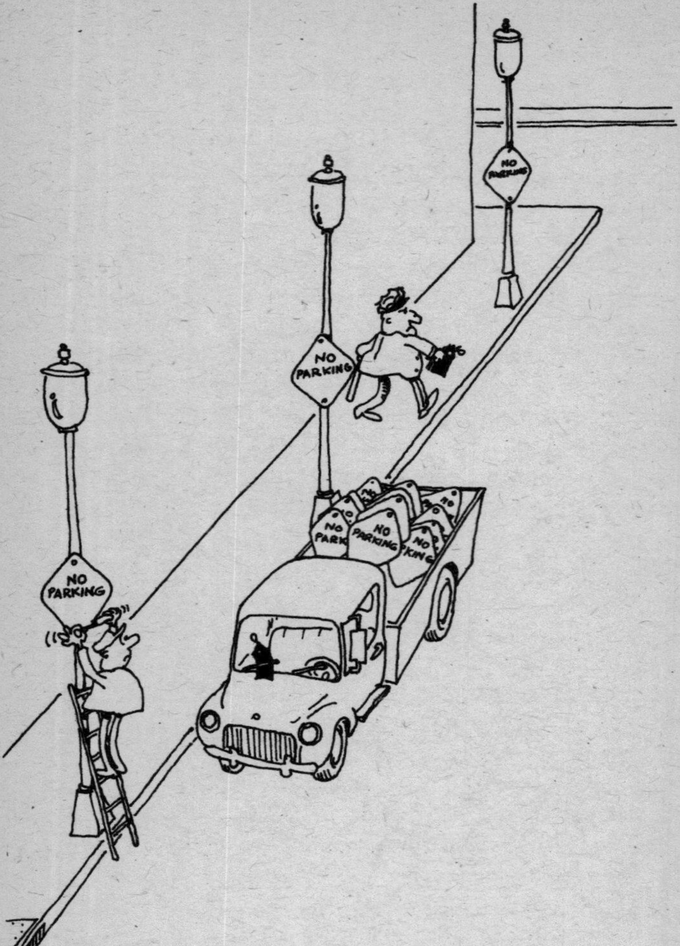
NO PARKING
NO PARKING
NO PARKING
NO PARK
NO PARKING

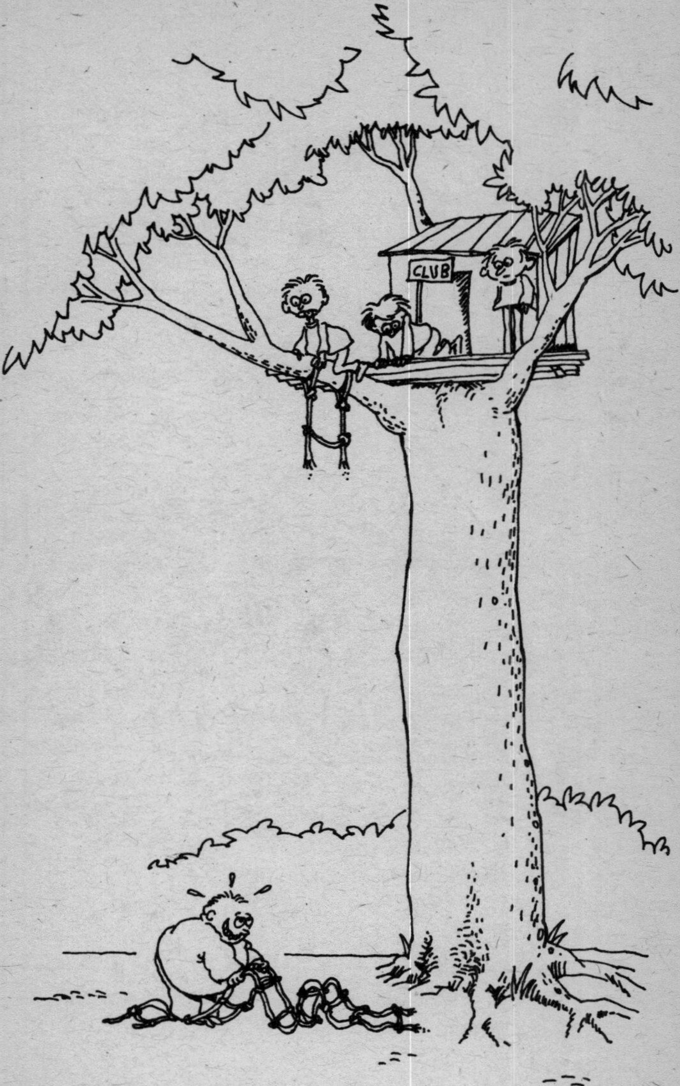
CLUB

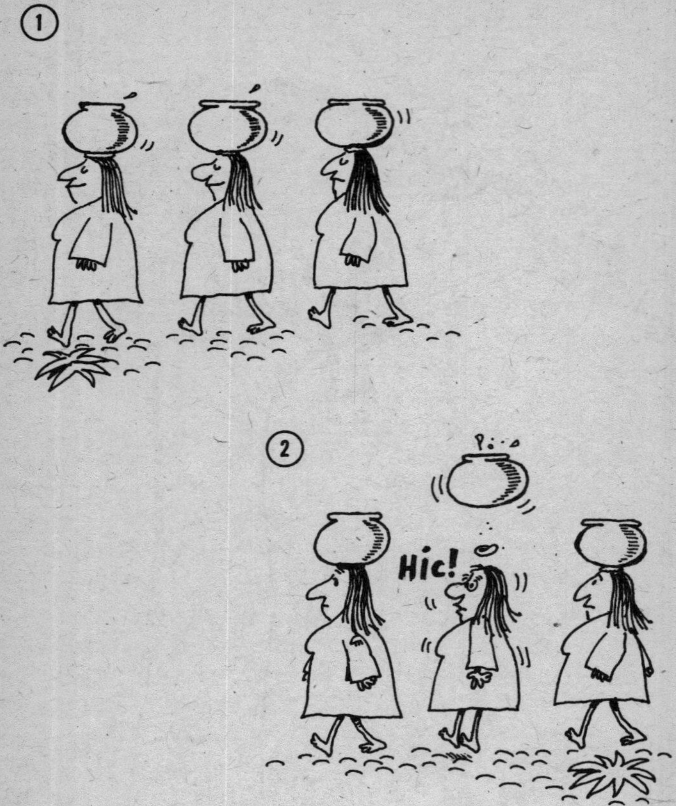
Hic!

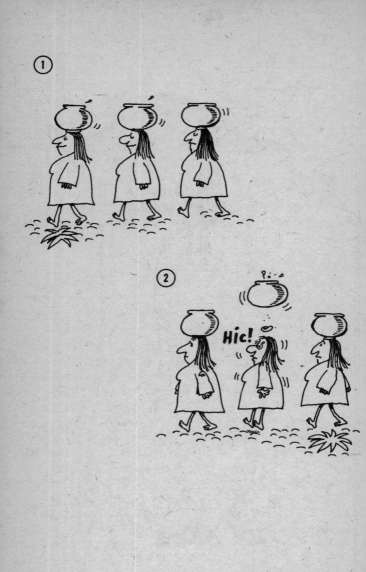

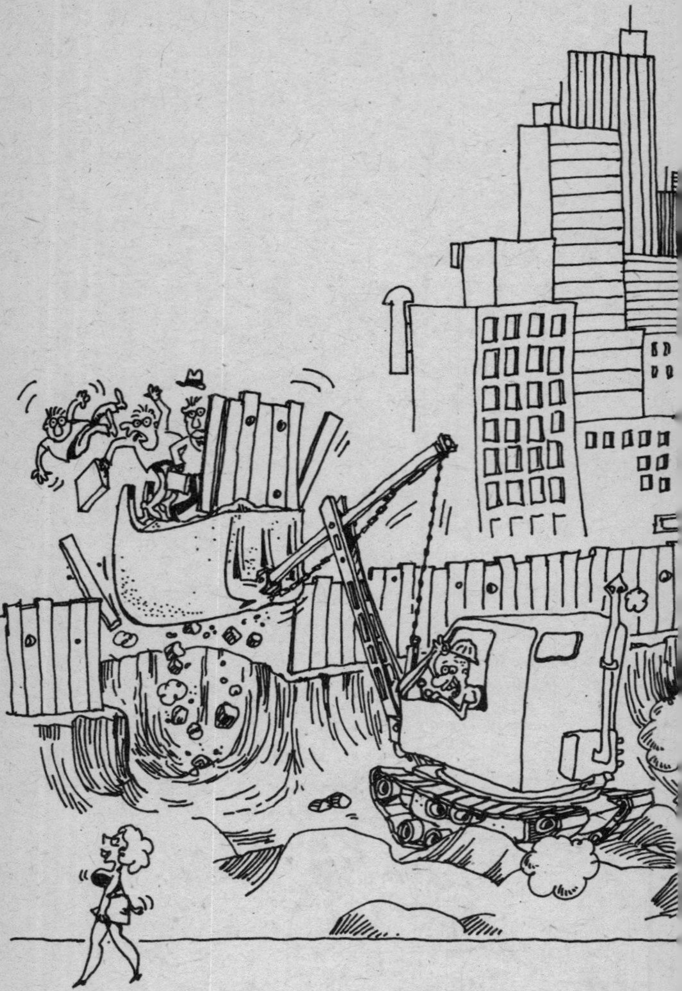

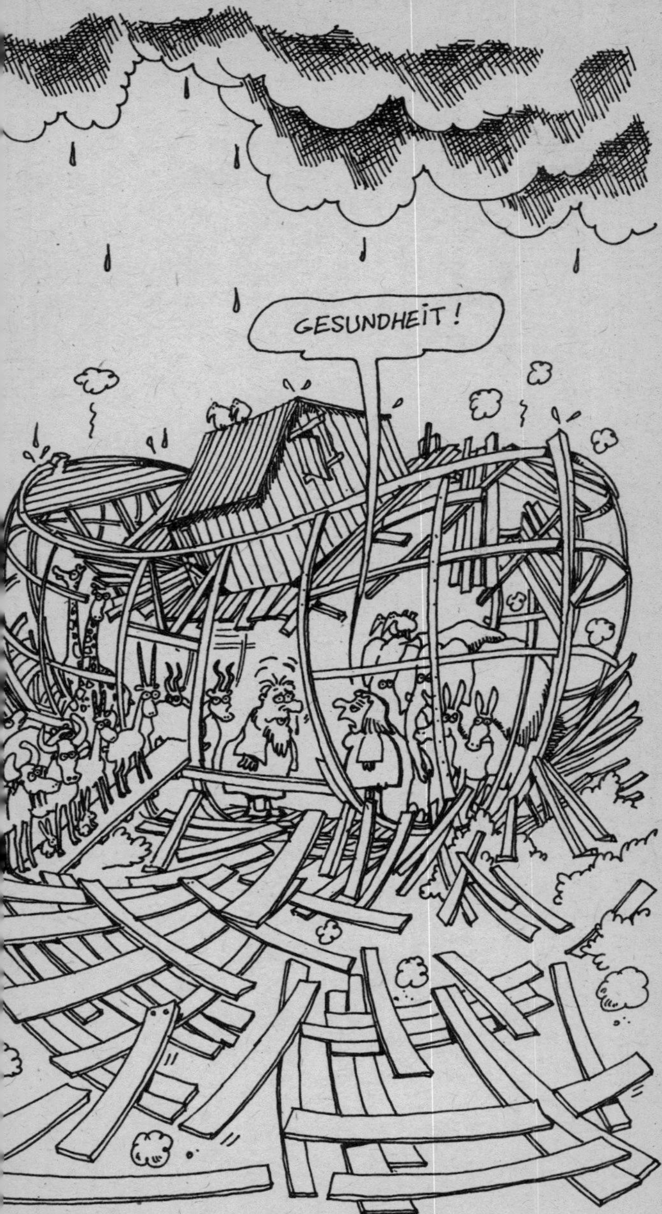
GESUNDHEIT!
SIFF

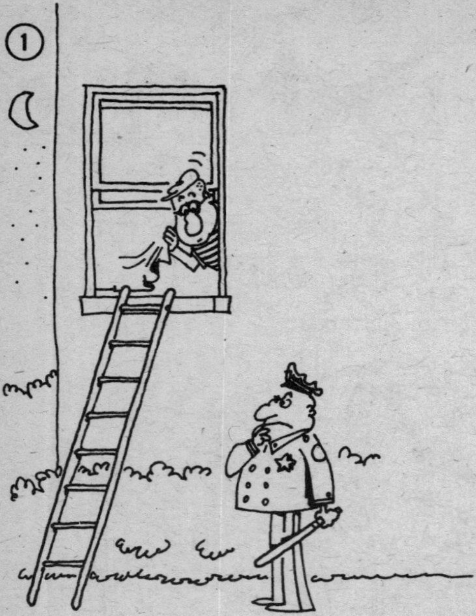
1

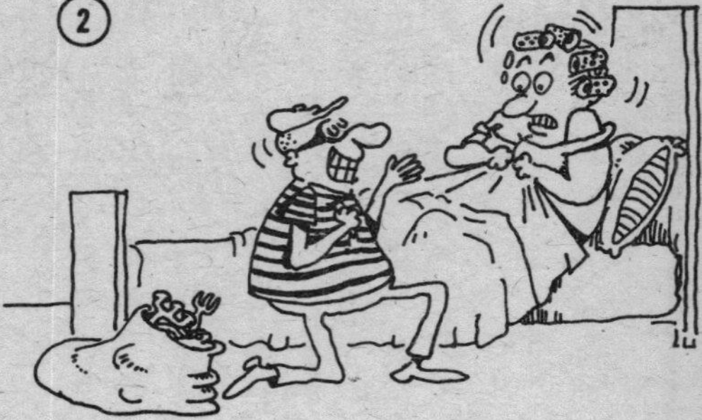
2

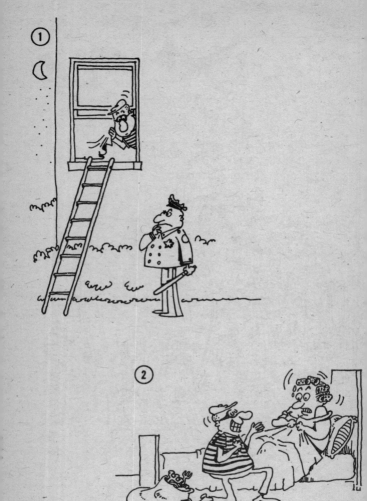

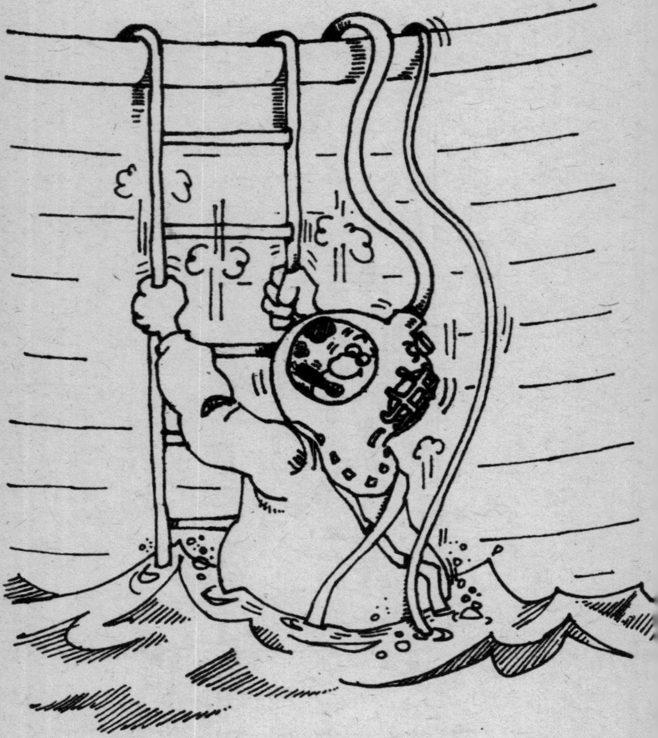

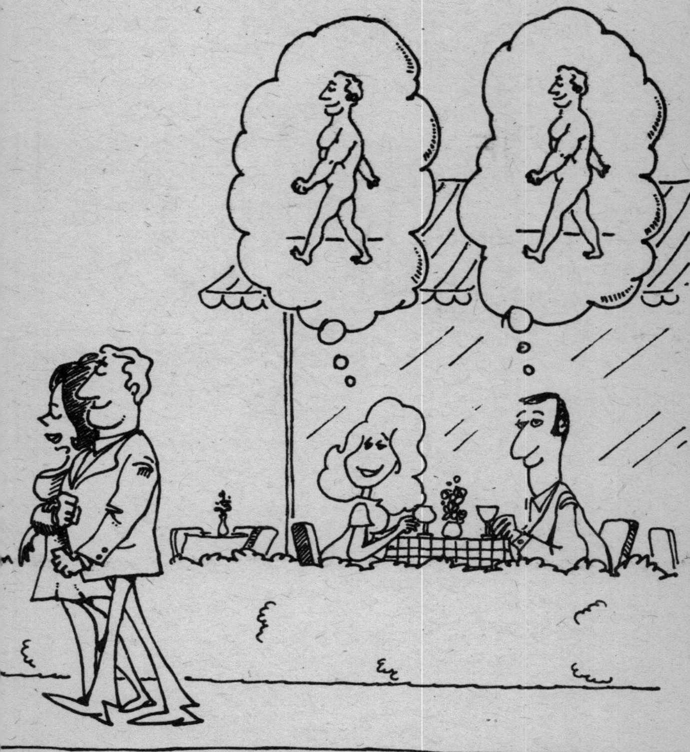

1

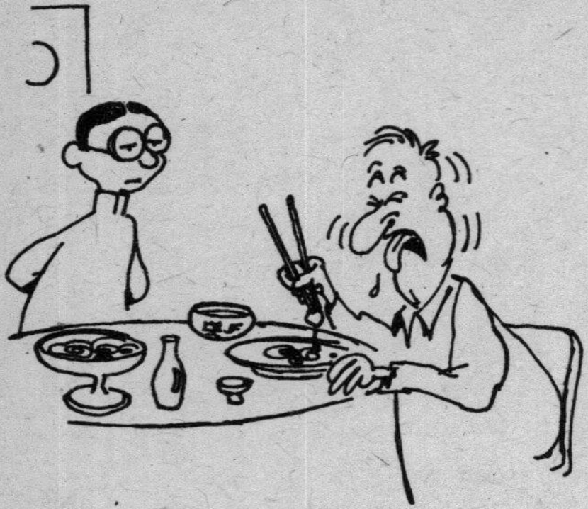

2

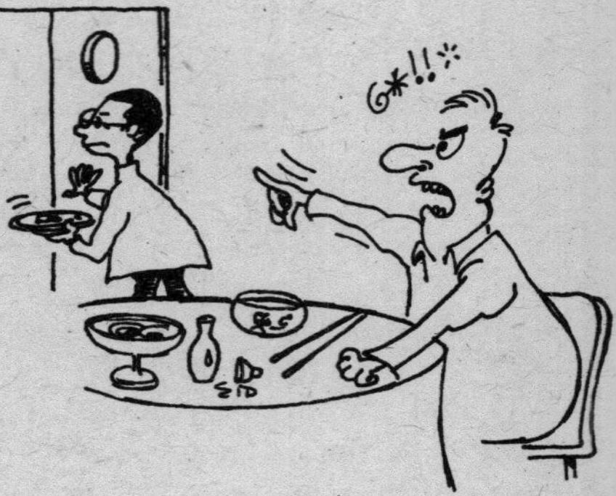
G*!!

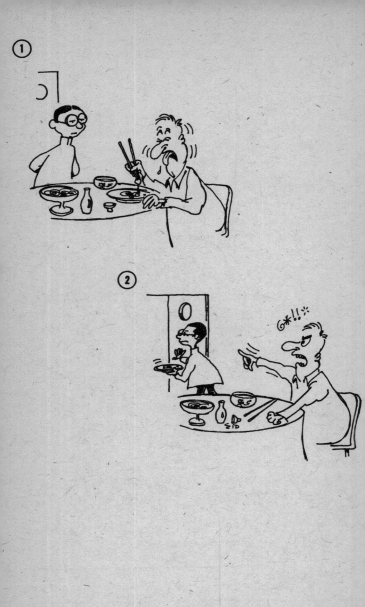

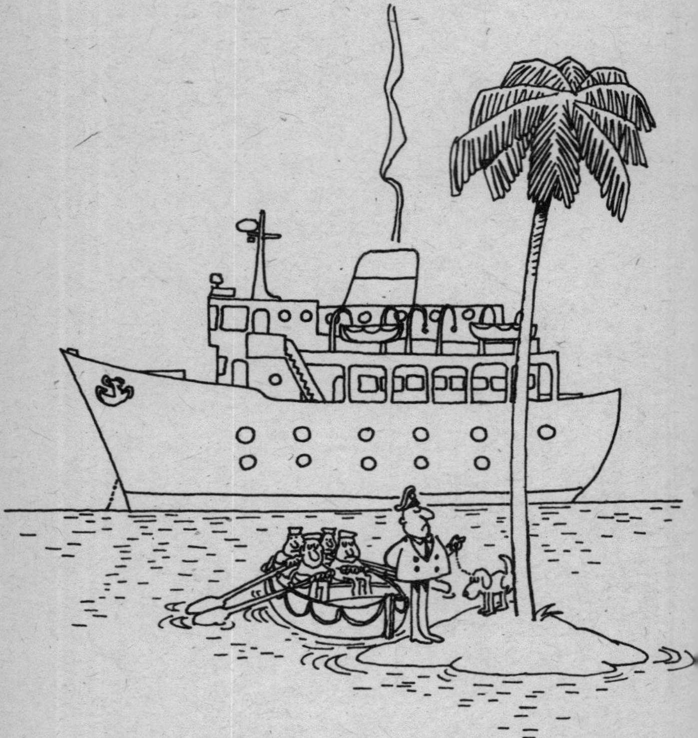

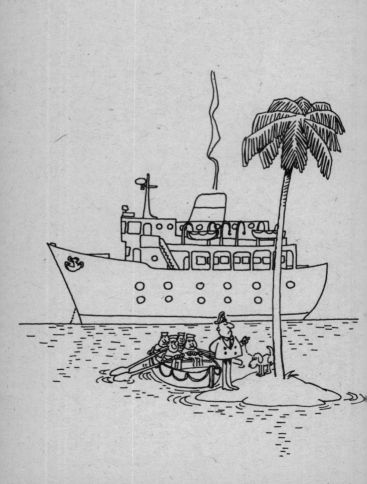

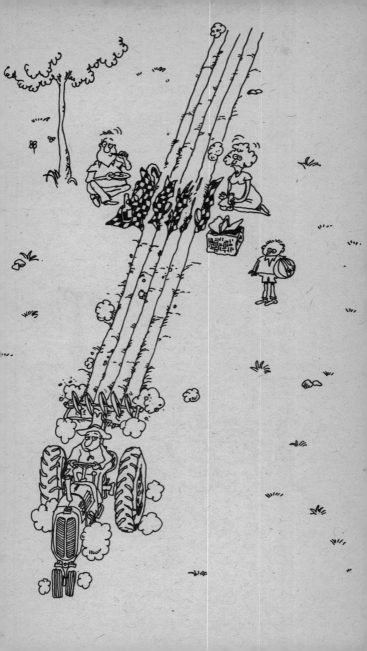

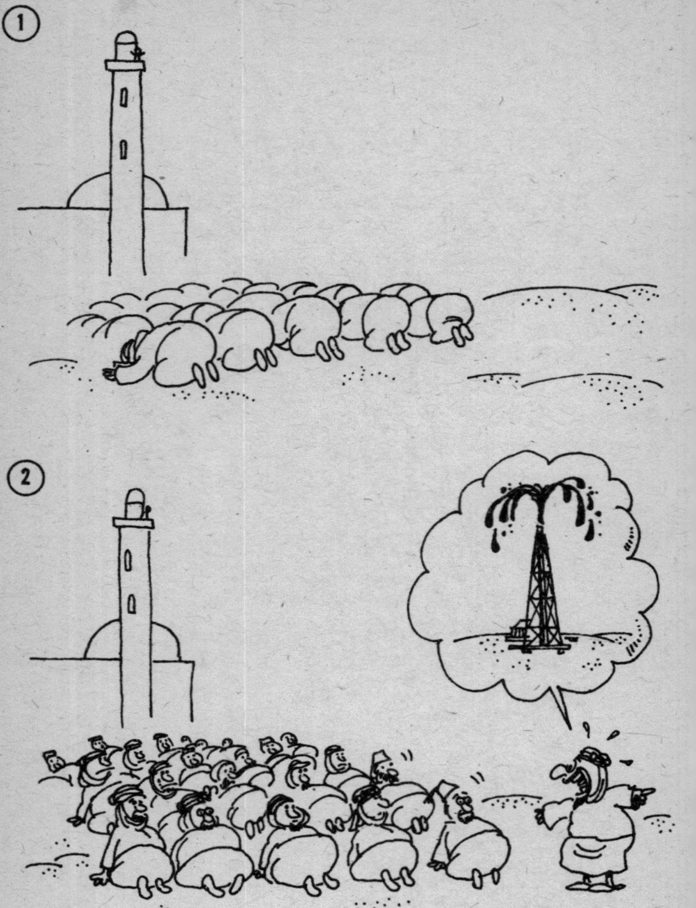
1
2

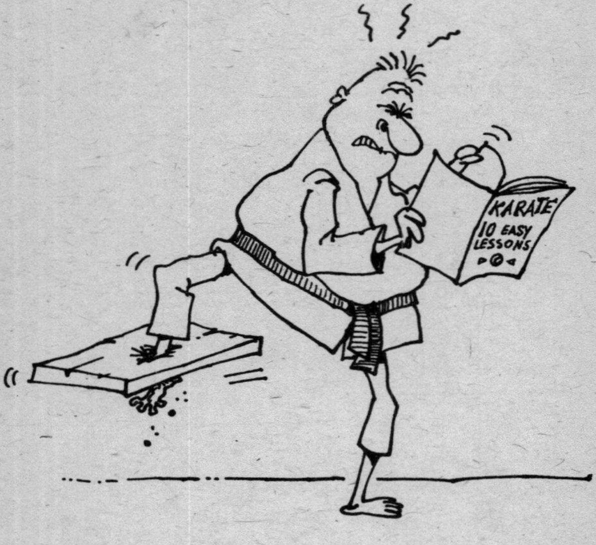
KARATE
10 EASY
LESSONS

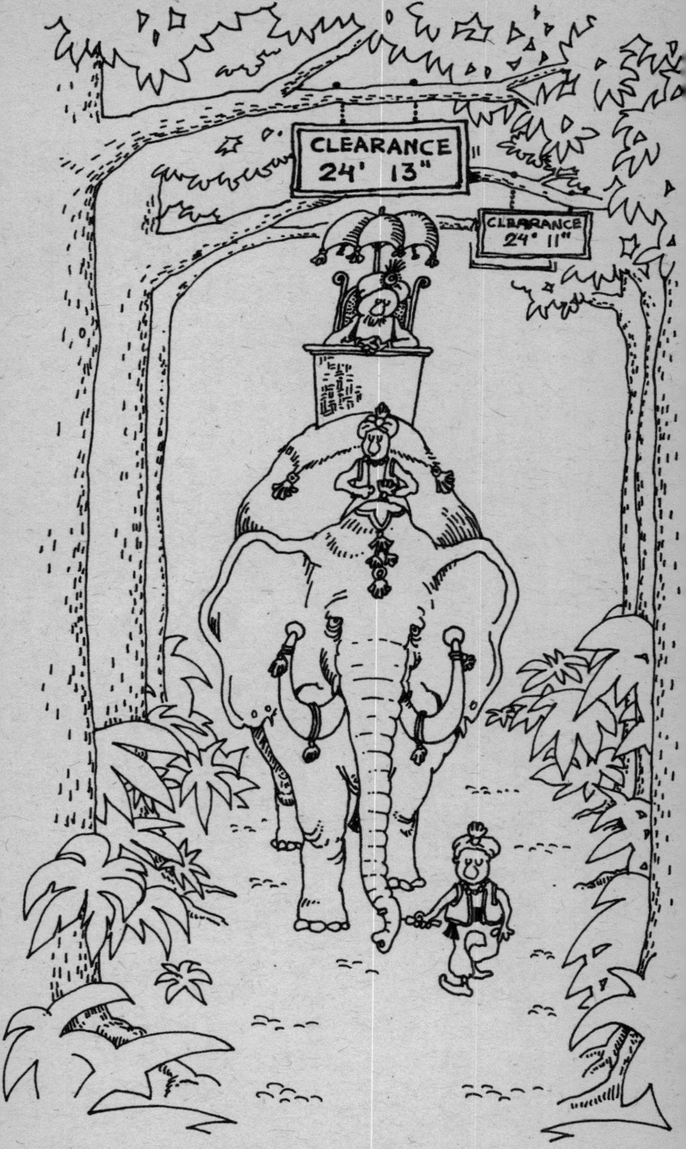
CLEARANCE
24' 13"
CLEARANCE
24' 11"

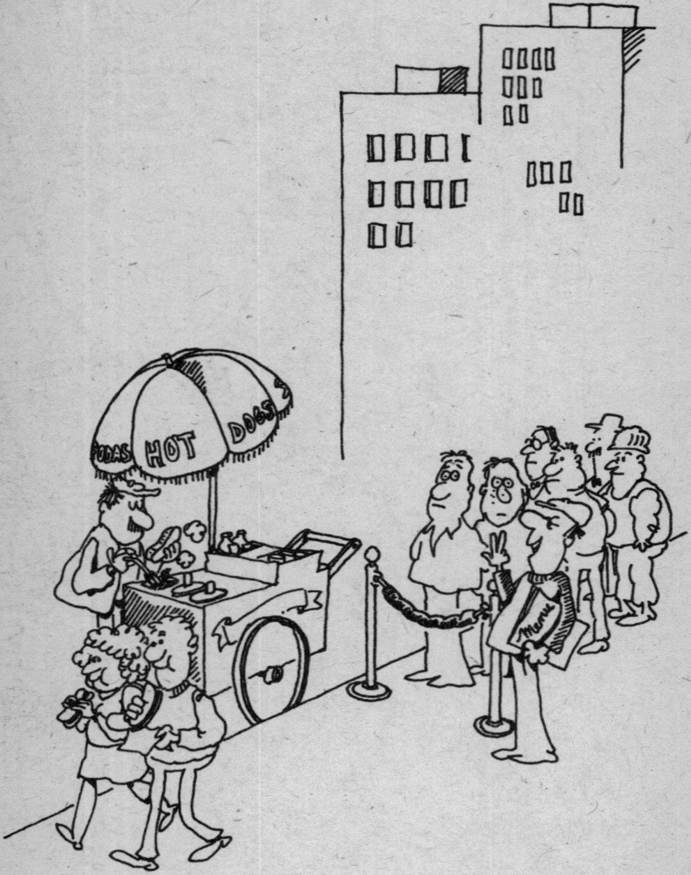
SODAS
HOT
DOGS

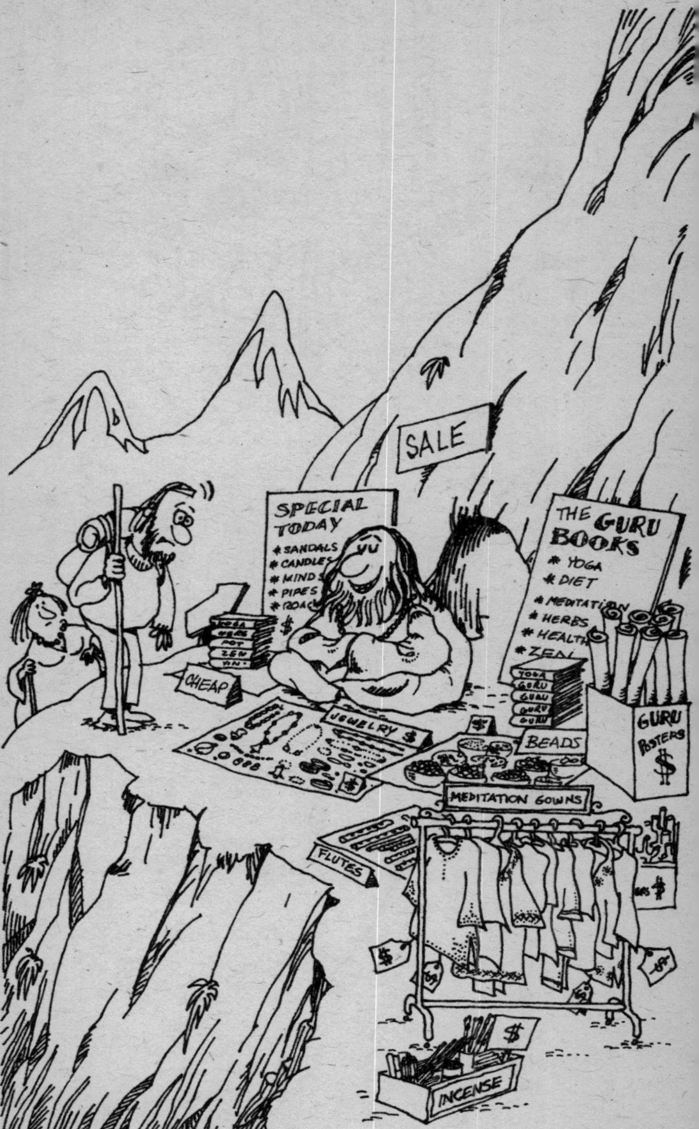
SALE
SPECIAL TODAY
* SANDALS
* CANDLES
* PIPES
$
YOGA
HERBS
POT
ZEN
YIN
CHEAP
THE GURU BOOKS
* YOGA
* DIET
* HERBS
YOGA
GURU
GURU
GURU
GURU
JEWELRY $
BEADS
GURU POSTERS $
MEDITATION GOWNS
FLUTES
INCENSE

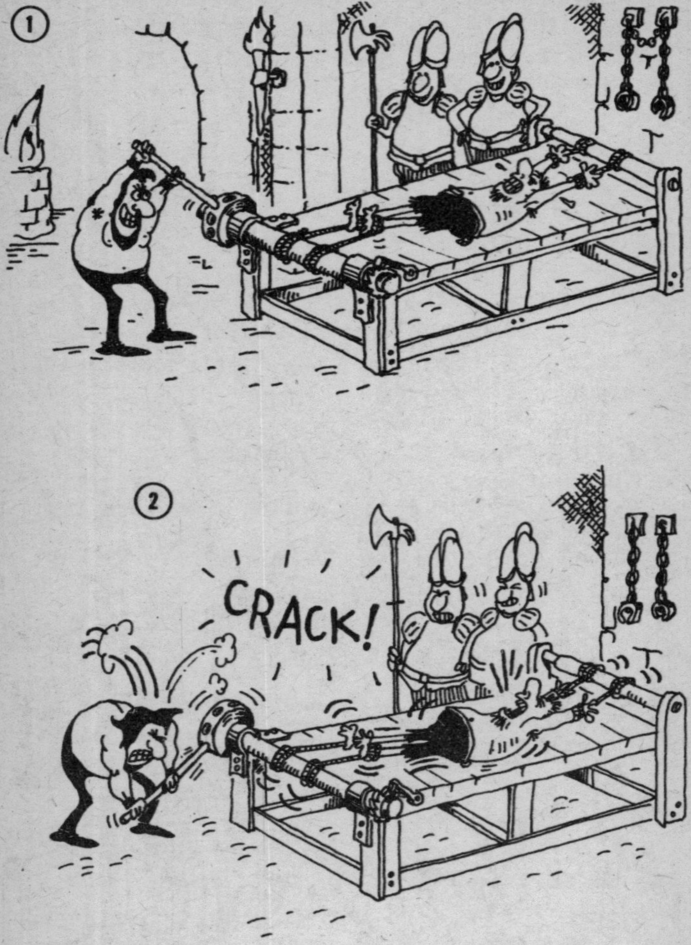
1
2
CRACK!

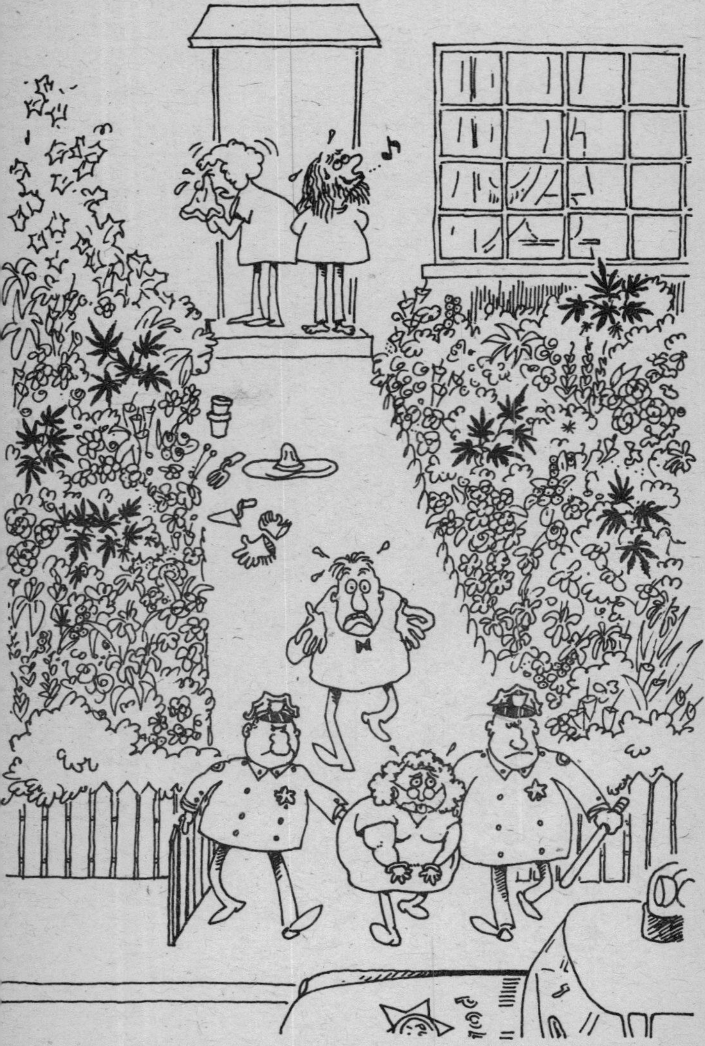

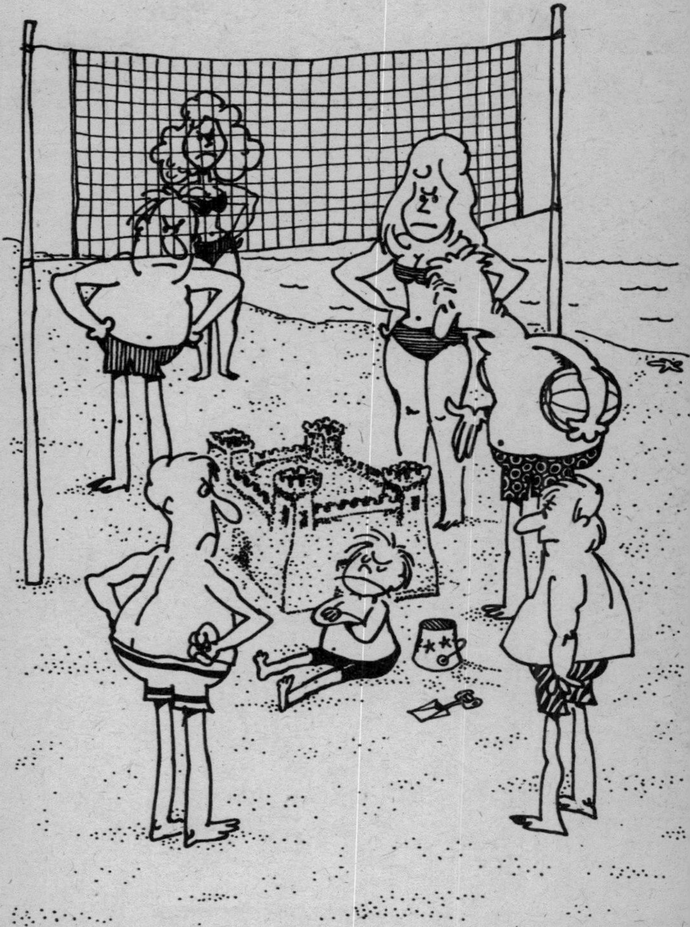

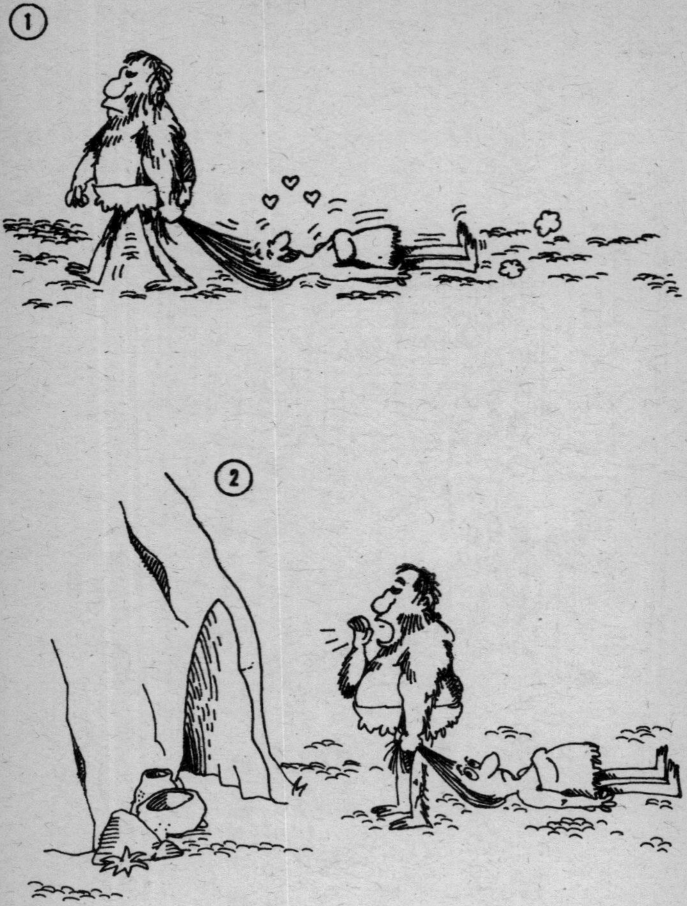
1
2

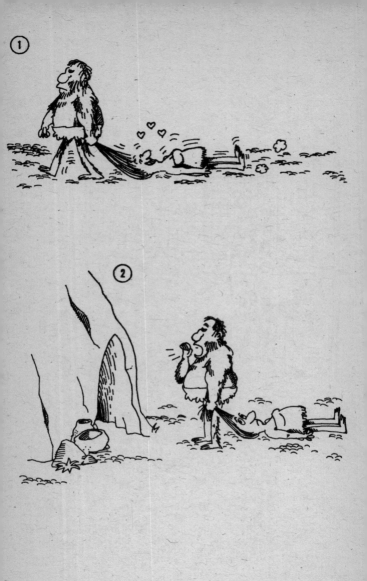

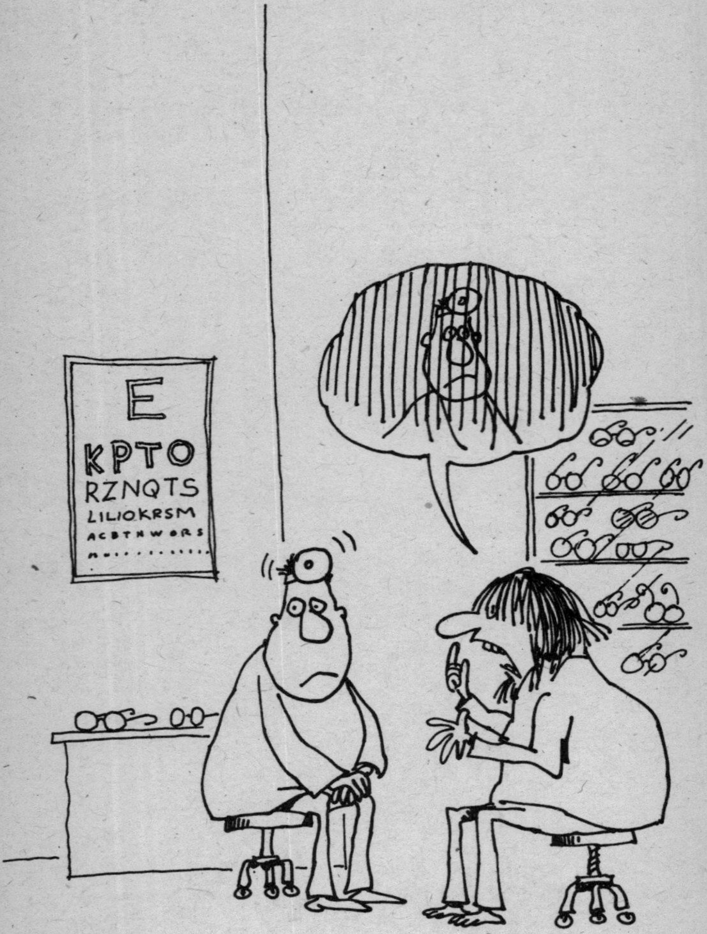
E
KPTO
RZNQTS
LILIOKRSM
ACBTHWORS

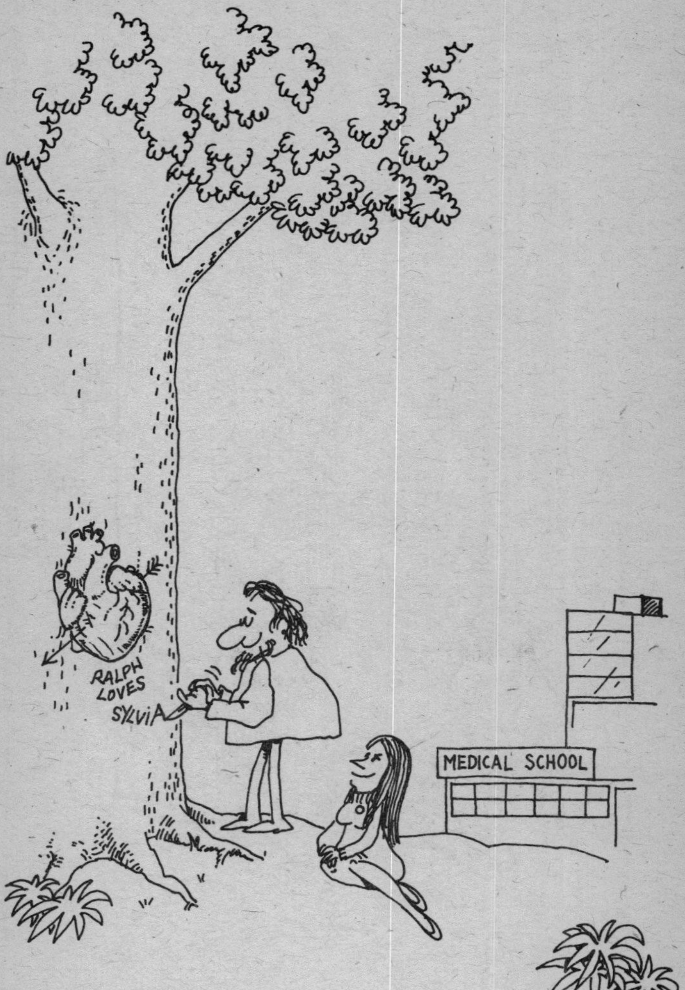
RALPH
LOVES
SYLVIA
MEDICAL SCHOOL

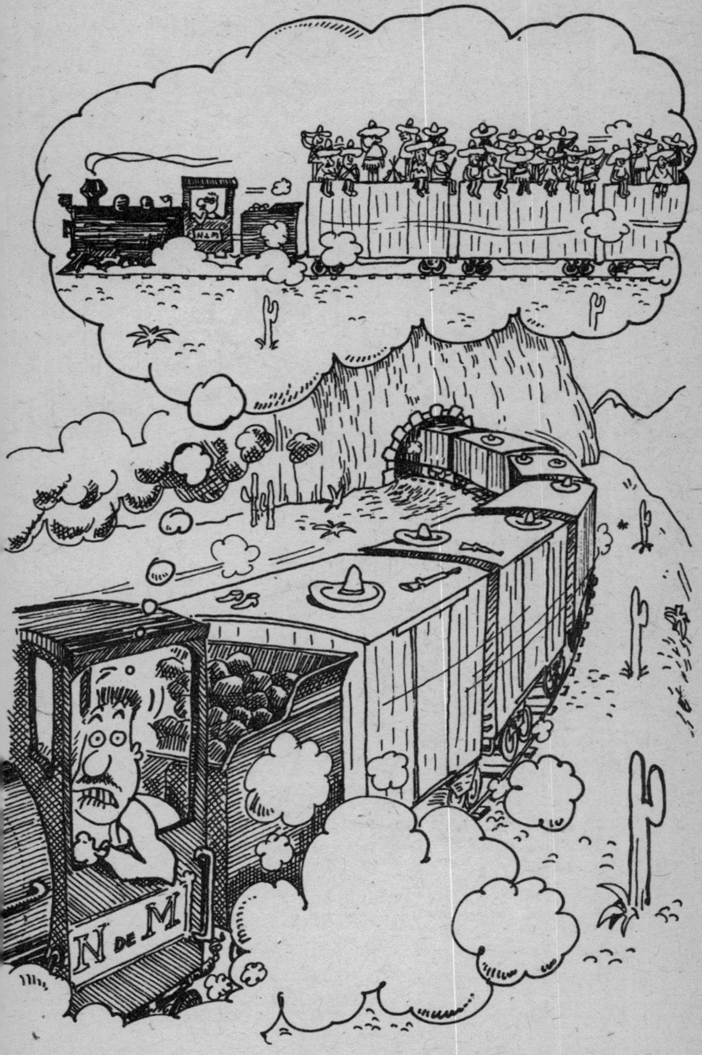
N DE M

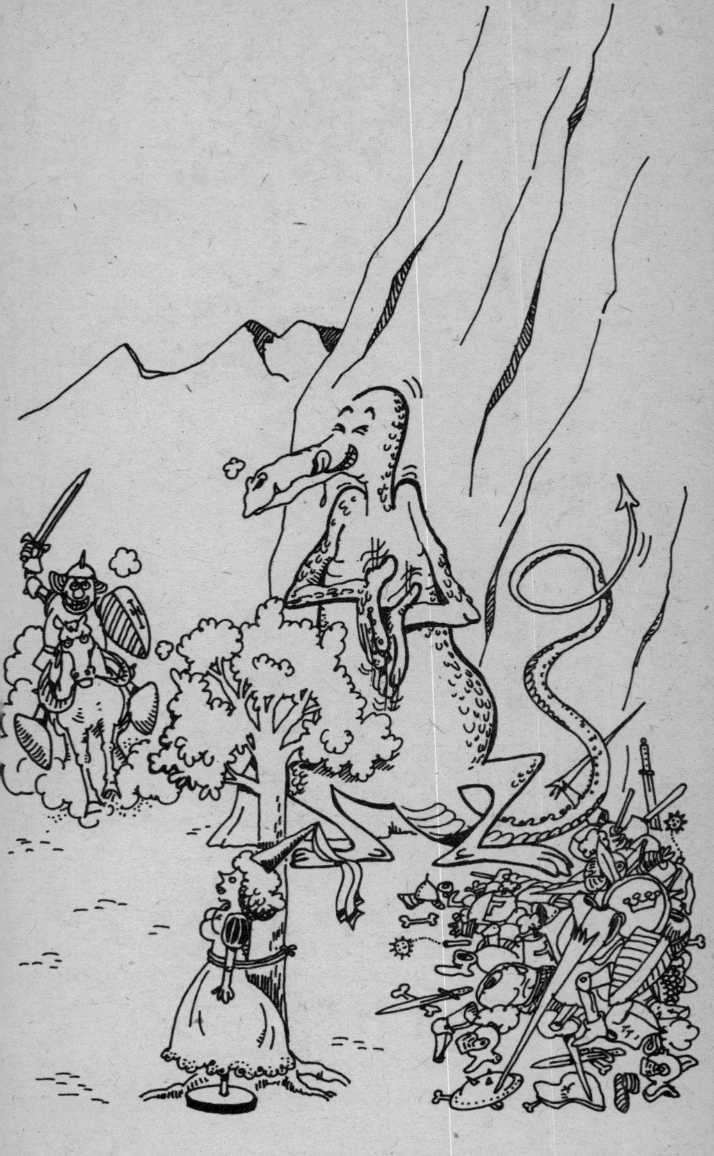

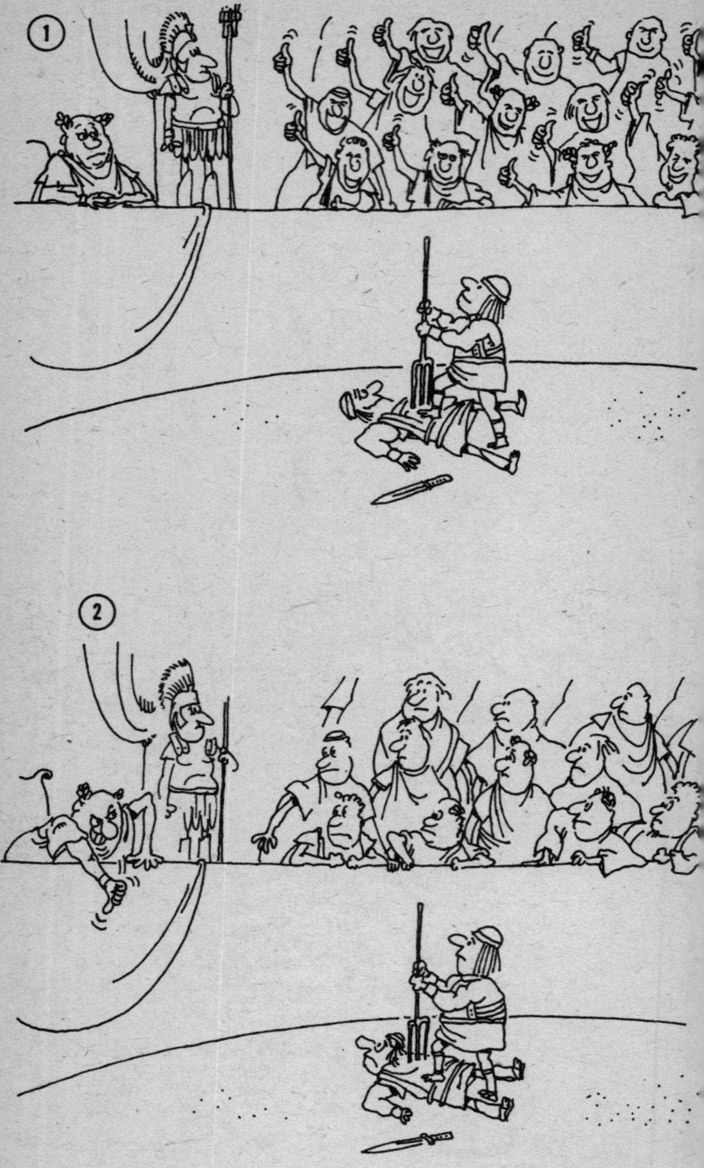
1
2

3

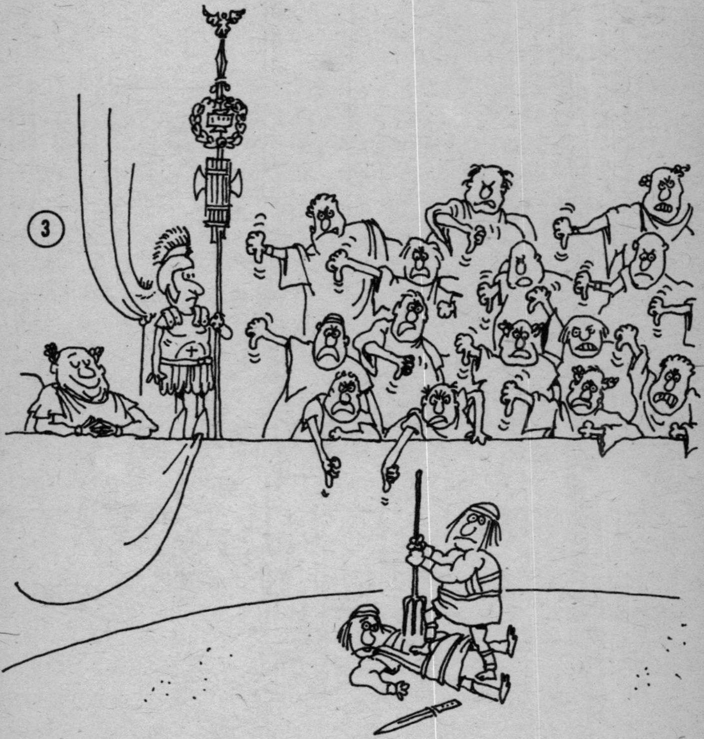

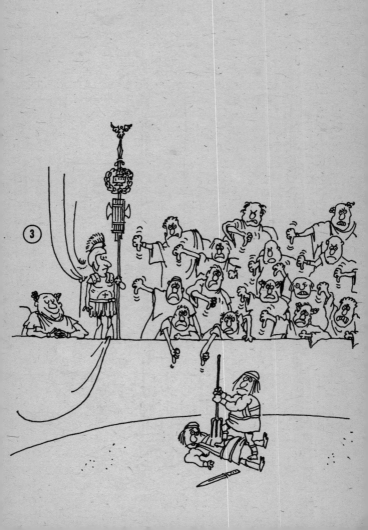

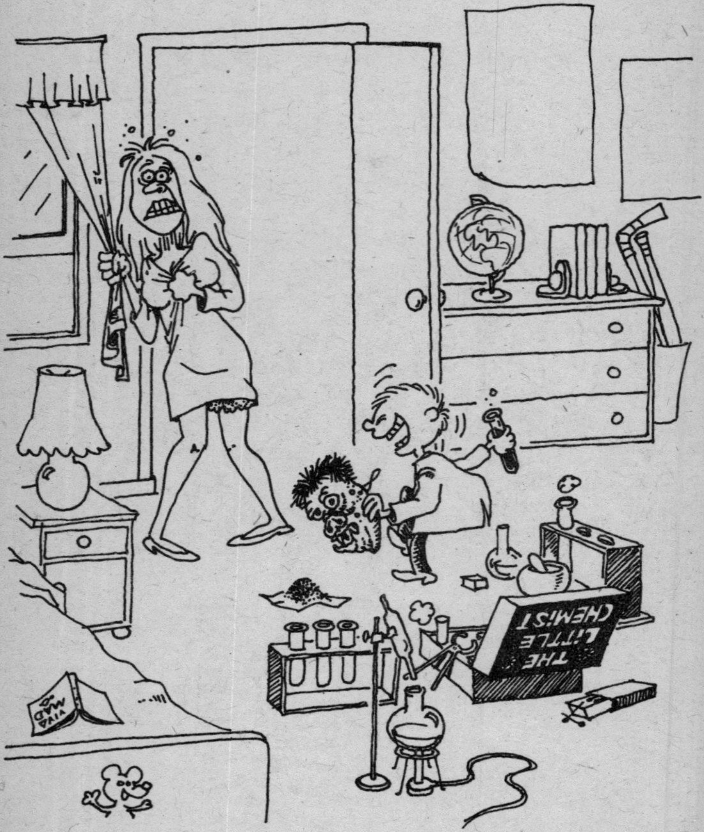
THE LITTLE CHEMIST
VIVA MAD

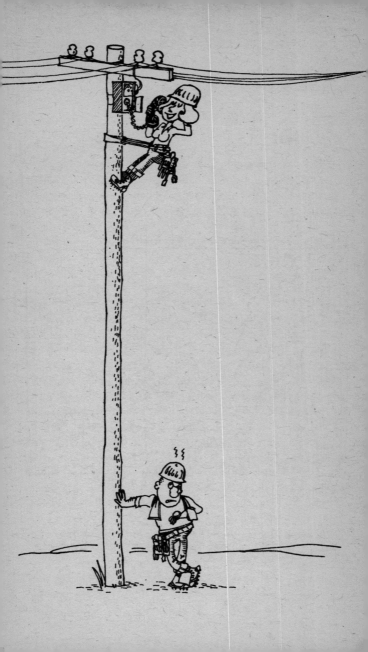

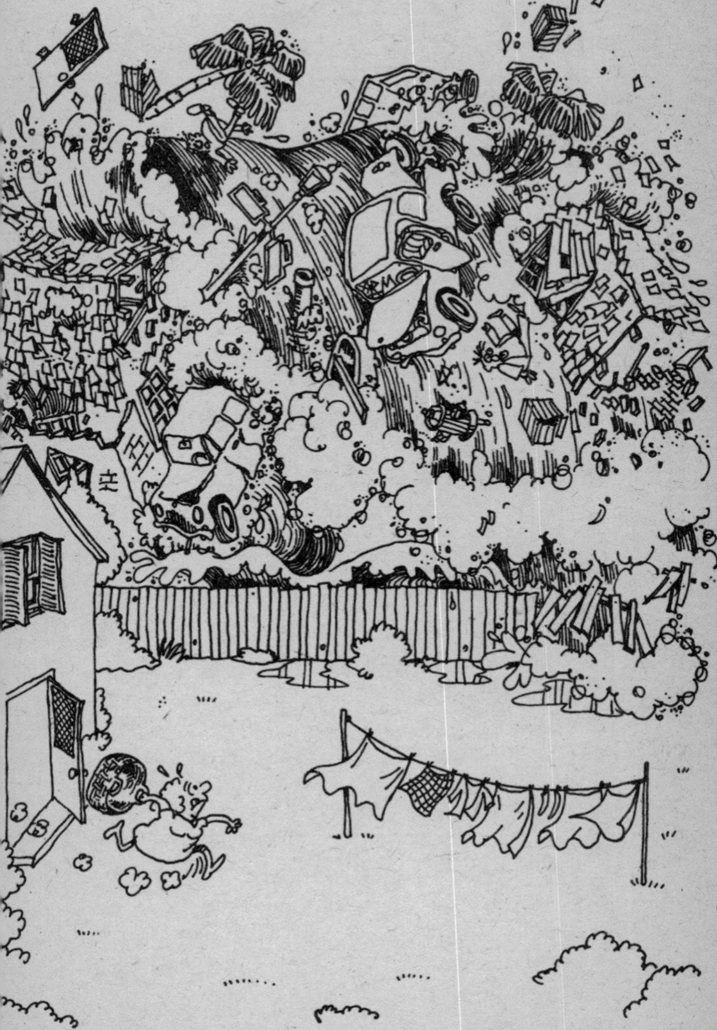

1

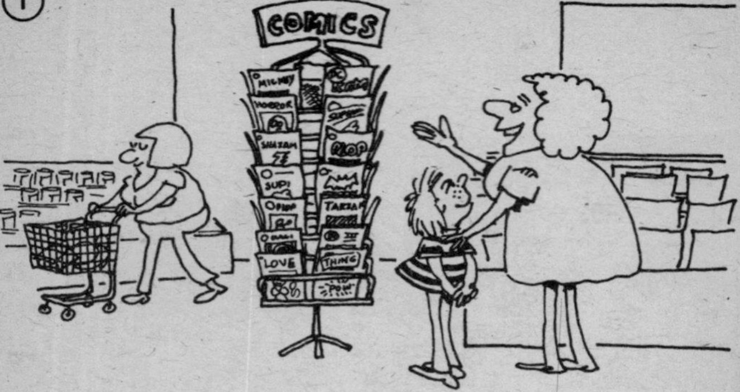
COMICS
HORROR
SHAZAM
SUPI
TARZAN
LOVE
THING
PLOP

2

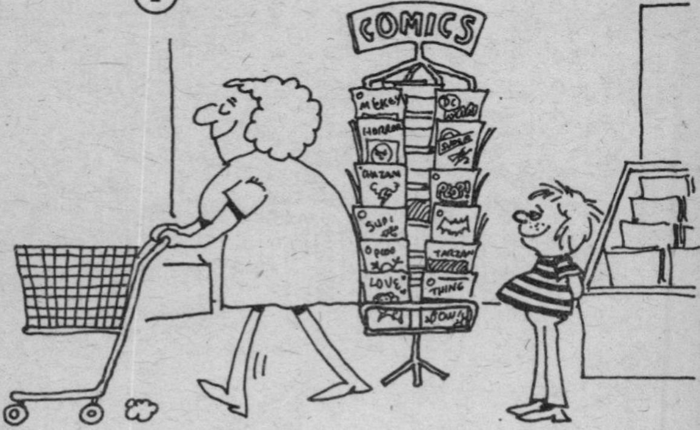
COMICS
HORROR
SUPI
TARZAN
LOVE
THING

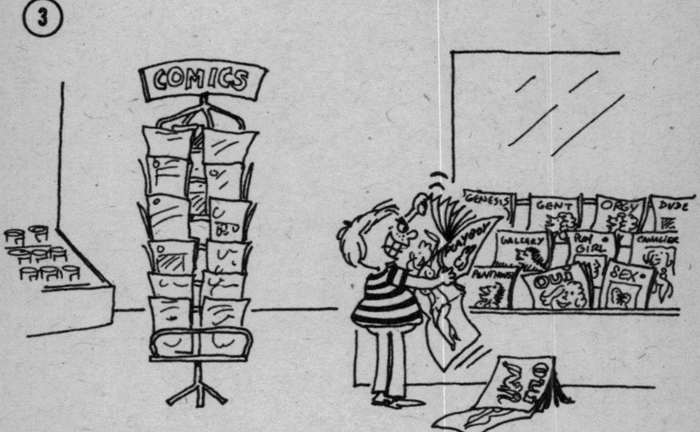
3
COMICS
GENESIS
GENT
ORGY
DUDE
PLAYBOY
GALLERY
PLAY GIRL
CAVALIER
PENTHOUSE
OUI
SEX
OUI

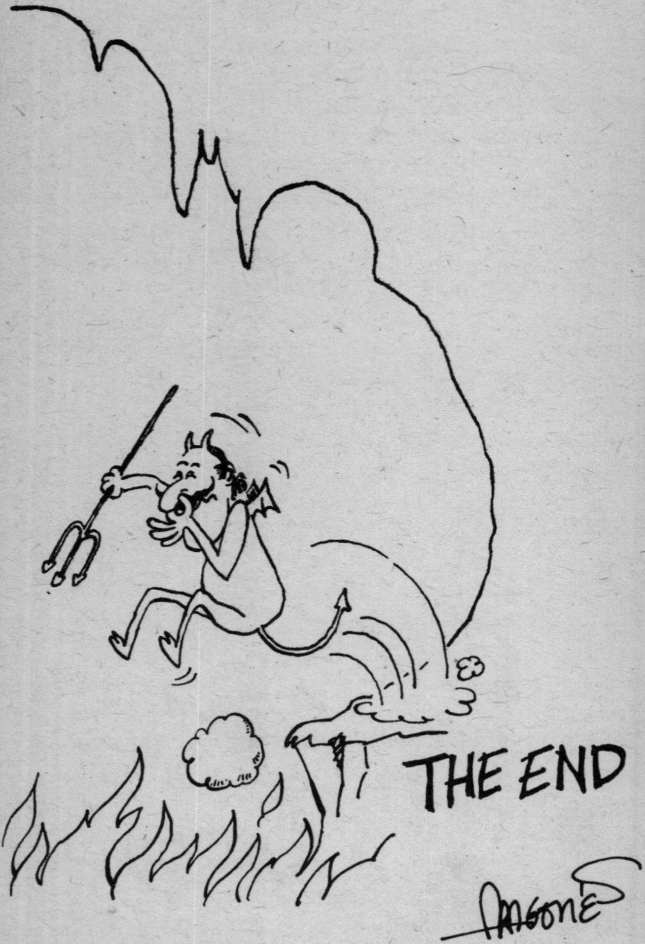
THE END